WILDLIFE IMAGES

A COMPLETE GUIDE TO OUTDOOR PHOTOGRAPHY

BY

JOHN WOOTTERS

AND

JERRY T. SMITH

Petersen Publishing Company, Los Angeles

*The bald eagle on the cover was photographed by Jerry T. Smith
in the Dallas zoo, using a 105mm Nikor
F3 body. Film was Kodachrome 64 exposed f/4 at 125.*

*Back cover, top, photographed by Jeanne Wootters;
bottom left, by Jerry T. Smith.*

Graphic Design by Dianne K. Moorman

Petersen Publishing Co., 8490 Sunset Blvd., Los Angeles, CA 90069

Library of Congress Catalog Card Number: 81-82706
ISBN 0-8227-3020-0 (Hardcover Edition)
ISBN 0-8227-3025-1 (Softcover Edition)

Printed in the United States of America

This book is dedicated to the
Professional Wildlife Managers of America.
Without these men and women,
wildlife in America might not be so abundant.
And, without wildlife, this book would
not have been possible.

Contents

Preface

Co-authoring a book is an interesting experience, especially for author Wootters who has written three books by himself in the past. It's especially interesting when the authors have widely differing photographic backgrounds and, in some areas, widely differing opinions about things. We believe the reader will actually benefit from these differences, but we also believe that he should understand the two authors' viewpoints.

Jerry Smith is a ''pure'' photographer, making most of his living with his camera. He sells prints of his own wildlife pictures, usually in limited editions, through his own art gallery in Alice, Texas, and occasionally through other galleries as well. His formal education is in art. Smith also sells wildlife photographs to various outdoor-oriented magazines, for illustrations and quite often for covers. As this is written, he has had more than 700 photos published, and about 75 covers, in the space of five years. He has been the subject of a television documentary and an article in *Southwestern Art* magazine, and is a favorite of many collectors of wildlife art.

All this has given him a distinct slant on equipment and films, as well as techniques. He's looking for the dramatic portrait of a species or a moment in the animal's life, recorded on fine-grain color film for the big enlargements usually needed in his work.

He also has access to many privately owned, wildlife-rich properties in south Texas and, within limits, more time than most of us can devote to field work.

John Wootters, on the other hand, is primarily a writer. Over a 20-year-plus career, he has had published more than 2½ million words on outdoor recreation topics, mostly hunting, fishing, nature study, photography, and sport shooting. It happens that in these fields a writer must also be a photographer, and, at a conservative estimate, Wootters has also had at least 10,000 pictures published. Not more than about 10 percent of these, however, have been wildlife photographs as such, and the great majority of them have been in black-and-white.

Because these published photos have almost all been *illustrations* of articles, Wootters has developed his own ideas about films, equipment, and techniques which differ from Smith's. The former is forever trying for a picture of an animal which illustrates some point about the species' behavior or relationship to mankind or its habitat. Whereas Smith needs a technically perfect portrait of a whitetail buck for a cover or an "edition," Wootters wants to show the buck doing something specific about which he intends to write, such as rubbing the velvet from his antlers or chasing a doe. He's willing to settle for a grainier film or one with less-than-perfect color rendition, or poor light, to catch the action when and where it happens.

Wootters' formal education was in English and journalistic photography. Perhaps the following sums up the distinctions in the two authors' ap-

Co-authors Wootters (left) and Smith plan a wildlife photography project from a tree platform in the game-rich brushlands of southern Texas. (Photo by Mike Alebis)

John Wootters waits for the moment in a wild animal's life he wishes to record.
(Photo by Jeanne Wootters)

Jerry Smith moves in for a macro close-up of a butterfly on a wildflower blossom.
(Photo by Mike Alebis)

proaches best: Jerry Smith is an artist, and John Wootters is a reporter.

This should not be mistaken for a ghost-written or "as-told-to" book, however. Wootters' qualifications as a wildlife photographer are, we believe, amply supported by the illustrations herein, and various sections of this manuscript were actually written by one or the other man, and so identified. The reader can interpret the sometimes differing viewpoints expressed in the light of the above sketches.

Lest too much be made of the differences, however, it should be noted that there exist even more similarities in the co-authors' approaches to wildlife photography. Both of us profoundly love the animals we seek to record on film. Both of us have been fascinated by wildlife from childhood, and neither of us could be entirely happy without a more-or-less constant association with wild animals and birds. Wootters has said that if he didn't have to make a living, wildlife photography is the activity to which he would devote his working hours, and Smith has made the same statement in his choice of a profession.

If it strikes a discordant note in the minds of some readers that Wootters is an avid hunter, those readers have simply demonstrated their own misconceptions of true hunters. Without discoursing upon the ethics of hunting, however, let it be pointed out that hunters, on the whole, learn a great deal about the habits of wild creatures and how to manipulate them, from the thousands of hours they spend annually in the field observing—not only game animals and birds, but nongame species as well. They also see and understand, better than most non-hunters, the harsh realities of the wild world, mentioned at greater length in the Introduction.

In fact, most of the tricks and methods of dealing with wildlife's early-warning system described in this book—such things as the use of camouflage, blinds, calls, scents, bait, and many others—are fundamental hunters' skills.

It's customary in the Preface for the author(s) to acknowledge the assistance of all those who contributed, directly or otherwise, to the work. In this case, both of us feel there are far too many to list them all, and too great a danger of leaving out someone who should have been included. They know who they are, however, and we hope they will accept our unspecified gratitude. Most of all, we are grateful to the occasional animal or bird which, in a moment of graceful forbearance, allowed us to record his image for all the human world to admire.

The dainty charm of a whitetail fawn sniffing a spring blossom radiates from this photo. (Photo by Jerry Smith)

John Wootters
Houston, Texas
May, 1981

Jerry Smith
Alice, Texas
May, 1981

Introduction

Most fine wildlife photographs result from one of two entirely different kinds of situations. The first is carefully planned and set up, often with a lot of fancy equipment (strobes, remote or automatic triggers, blinds, bait, etc.) and days or even weeks may be spent at the project before the exposure is made.

In the second kind of situation, the photographer simply sees something beginning to happen and seizes the opportunity. This kind of shot requires of the cameraman a fine sense of timing and an almost unconscious familiarity with his camera.

Both situations demand of the photographer a thorough understanding of the temperament and habits of the species being photographed. The planned setup must be thought out in light of the expected reaction of the creature to the situation, and the "grab-shot" artist has to know his quarry well enough to predict what is about to happen next. In neither case will luck play a very important role, sad to say.

And that will be, we hope, what sets this book apart from most of those on our subject already in print. We will deal with equipment and lenses and films, of course, but we are determined to try to teach the reader *how one goes about getting close enough to wild creatures to use those fancy lenses and fast films.*

It must also be understood that this is a book on *wildlife* photography, and not on *nature* photography. Our topic is photographing living creatures; we shall omit the sections on landscapes, flower photography, sunsets, beach scenes, etc. Our range is from insects to elephants (not excluding fish).

Furthermore, we shall assume the reader enjoys a basic understanding

This kind of wildlife picture, of a big whitetail buck sailing over a fence in a dense fog, can never be planned. It results from the photographer's willingness to be out there in the fog, despite the poor prospects, on the alert and ready to seize the opportunity when it presents itself.
(Photo by John Wootters)

of the principles of photography, and that he or she is sufficiently serious about photographing wildlife that quality equipment can be worked into the budget. We might like to tell you that prize-winning wildlife photos can be taken with pocket-sized automatic cameras in the 110 format, but we cannot, in good faith. Wildlife photography is one of the most demanding specialties in the photographic field, and at least some specialized equipment is a necessity. This doesn't mean, however, that very expensive, professional grade cameras and lenses are required; it goes without saying that the better the gear the better the results are likely to be, but there are many moderately priced camera systems available today with which excellent work can be done.

The key word there is "system;" the authors (who, by the way, do not use the same brands of equipment and disagree on many things) do feel that it would be a disservice to the reader to encourage him to think that anything less than a decent 35 mm single-lens reflex with interchangeable lenses and a few accessories will enable him to produce great wildlife pictures.

On the other hand, we would encourage him to think that he can produce great wildlife pictures without traveling to Africa or Yellowstone Park. Fine, dramatic, storytelling wildlife pictures can be taken in your backyard, the city park, the zoo, and elsewhere locally. Several of the photos reproduced in this book, in fact, were taken in the authors' backyards.

Wherever he works, the wildlife photographer must assume certain responsibilities, in our view, responsibilities both to the wild creatures and to the human society to which he represents those creatures.

He must avoid any action which might cause harm to the wildlife. Frightening a brooding bird away from her nest can destroy her entire year's reproductive contribution to her species. Frightening a yarded deer into running as little as 100 yards in deep snow in February can seal its death warrant, so precariously balanced are its energy resources at that time of year. Forcing a reptile to remain in direct sunlight for only ten minutes may be fatal to the subject. Cornering a wild animal creates a sort of desperate terror in which it may injure itself or trample its young. Such things are often done in all innocence, but they remain inexcusable.

Many species are extremely sensitive to disturbance of the habitat, especially during denning and young-rearing periods. The responsible photographer has the job of knowing and respecting these characteristics, as well as of avoidance of any detrimental alteration of the habitat, by cutting trees or whatever.

If he implements a winter feeding plan to attract birds and animals for the camera, he must assume responsibility for maintaining availability of food

Jerry Smith, in camouflage in the foreground, has used his insight into the nature and habits of wild turkey gobblers to stalk within easy camera range of this strutting male. (Photo by Mike Alebis)

John Wootters spotted these infant bobcats in a low tree and walked a mile to and from his vehicle to get a camera and telephoto for this shot. A closer approach or any effort to clear away the intervening brush might have frightened the babies and separated them from their mother, so the author settled for this view to avoid the possibility of harm to the kittens. (Photo by John Wootters)

A great deal of wildlife photography can be done in familiar places close to home, in city parks and suburbs, and even in the photographer's backyard, as was the case with this gray squirrel. (Photo by John Wootters)

The authors feel that the wildlife photographer must be objective. A coyote can be shown as a villain, a destroyer of innocent deer fawns, or as one more species within an ecosystem, going about his daily business. (Photo by John Wootters)

Habitat modifications to suit the convenience of the photographer must be done judiciously. Here, author Smith carefully trims away foliage around a mourning dove's nest to provide a clear prospect for the lens. (Photo by Mike Alebis)

Although not a popular subject on African photographic safaris, these Egyptian vultures are very much a part of life on the veldt and tell a story of life as it really is as they scrabble over a fresh carcass. (Photo by John Wootters)

throughout the winter stress period, even when inconvenient; a songbird which has become habituated to a feeder may not migrate and will die if food is not provided.

Finally, there are some species which are certainly the rarest of camera trophies but which are so critically endangered that they should be spared even the most benign of human interventions.

To the society in which he lives, the wildlife photographer has the responsibility to carry an "honest camera," seeing to it that his pictures represent reality. It is our opinion that we have had quite enough of nature-faking, beginning decades ago with "Bambi" (perhaps the most contemptible literary example of anthropomorphism) and proceeding through a generation of similar works both literary and cinematic, specifically including some of the Disney produced wildlife epics. The wildlife photographer always stands an an interpreter, as well as a reporter, between the wild world and the human society, even if he shows his pictures only to a few friends and family. Wildlife desperately needs the understanding of mankind, but it can be valuable only if it's a realistic understanding.

Every wild creature lives in constant danger, competition, and stress. He suffers the threat of drought, famine, winterkill, predators, and parasites the year around. His essential habitat may be squeezed dangerously by the works of man, his food supplies destroyed, and his numbers reduced perilously near the point of reproductive "critical mass." A minor injury or infection which, in a domestic animal, would represent nothing more than a small veterinarian's bill, is often fatal. There is no escape from pain, disability, starvation, cold, windstorms, or snow for most wild animals. It's no easy life, and the fact that species do survive and thrive is a mark of their incredible, but often not obvious, toughness and ability simply to endure.

All these things can be shown in pictures. Perhaps the most telling protests against oceanic oil spills ever made were the pictures of pathetic, doomed, oil-soaked seabirds. Those cameramen were serving both the wildlife and the society by turning their lenses on such painful subjects.

This is not to say that the wildlife photographer must seek out scenes of death and agony in the name of realism. Most wildlife pictures properly reflect the beauty of healthy creatures in harmony with their environment, triumphant over the hardships with which they live every day, and this is an equally valid message. But the lines are hard to draw. Lions do kill and eat innocent baby zebras; snakes do eat helpless toads (without killing first). A necessity for survival for the lion or snake is the final tragedy for the zebra foal or toad. Nature is merciless at every level, and the knowing photographer will see it all, a magnificent machine functioning according to timeless rhythms. If he selects only the pleasant and pretty to record, his record will

An elephant cow charges the photographer to protect her calf. A dramatic picture, but the author was at fault for approaching the group closely enough to disturb the cow this badly. This charge was serious, not a bluff, which also points up the possibility of real danger in working around large animals. (Photo by John Wootters)

be no more truthful than if he chose only the violent and bloody scenes.

It isn't easy, but the only satisfactory approach is complete objectivity. If the snake is seen as evil, or the coyote as a villain, if there are protagonists and antagonists in the photographer's mind, they will be there in his negatives and slides as well. The greatest wildlife photographers have always been those who could learn to see and accept the workings of the wild world. That world has no human emotions or value systems and, in fact, is monumentally indifferent to such abstractions.

The photographer, professional or amateur, who can accept that fact is on his way to a truly honest portrayal of nature—and to fulfillment of his inherent responsibilities.

1

What Makes A Good Wildlife Photograph?

As soon as the technology of photography was developed to at least a primitive approximation of that of today, people began to turn their lenses on wild animals. The oldest volume in author Wootters' collection of books on this subject was published in 1924 and is entitled *Stalking Big Game With a Camera.* It was written and illustrated by a gentleman named Marius Maxwell, whom we presume to have been a well-to-do Englishman, and deals exclusively with the large and often dangerous game of Africa, especially elephants.

Even Maxwell was not the first, of course. He acknowledges his debt to two authors who photographed African game before him, one C. G. Schillings, a German whose first book with game photographs appeared in 1905, and another Britisher, Radclyffe Dugmore, who published a book entitled *Camera Adventures in the African Wilds* somewhat later. We have no records of wildlife photography volumes of that era devoted to domestic species; the world was in love with Africa in those bygone days.

In reading Maxwell's treatise, a modern photographer will be struck with the basic similarity of the problems he faced with our own, especially by his complaints about the slowness of telephoto lenses and the sensitivity of film emulsions to heat, both of which will be dealt with in the present volume. He was also plagued with the matter of weight and handiness in his equipment. He considered a 4x5-inch glass plate or film negative a "miniature" and was terribly proud of achieving an exposure as short as 1/100th with a 4X telephoto (equivalent of a 200 mm in modern 35 mm camera terms). He described his favorite camera as ". . . built of well-seasoned teakwood with the joints free from glue, being either dovetailed or screwed," and

Notice the terrific diagonal upward thrust of action in this shot of snow geese taking flight. Sometimes it's possible to fill a whole frame with this dynamic feeling, as in this case. Study the various wing positions in this picture long enough and you may actually imagine that you see them move, so forceful is the action.
(Photo by John Wootters)

Patience is one of the great virtues of a wildlife photographer. Here, Jerry Smith waits patiently at a waterhole for thirsty wildlife to appear. Like infantry combat, wildlife photography is about 99 hours of boredom punctuated with a minute or two of frantic action. (Photo by Mike Alebis)

advised covering the woodwork with leather to render it less conspicuous, ". . . and the fittings lacquered or painted in such a way as to blend with colours of the particular environment for which it is to be used." We will have more to say about camouflaging a camera a little further along.

Maxwell's camera had a bellows and maximum focal length of 25 inches with his pet lens, giving a 2.5X magnification and effective aperture of f/10 at best.

If we could have handed this brave fellow a Nikon with a 400 mm, f/3.5 lens, loaded with Kodachrome 64, he would probably have fainted dead away for joy!

He tells us nothing of his processing, except to mention at one point that he should have used a cold water bath to harden a heat-softened emulsion, but we are left to assume that he processed his precious film-packs in a tent at night in the African wilderness. *That* must have been a nice task!

Yet he got some very good pictures, at times literally at the risk of life and limb, snapping away and ripping the tabs off his film-packs as an elephant or rhino charged down on him. When we are inclined to complain about our "hardships" in the course of modern wildlife photography, a quick rereading of the works of such pioneers as Maxwell and Dugmore and the American George Shiras (who will be mentioned again) will lend us a fresh perspective.

The photographs of animals taken by these men were heroic achievements under the circumstances, but the fact is that most of them would not get past the secretary of the first assistant to the deputy associate art director of any magazine in publication today. We cannot measure their work against the standards for quality today, nor can we forgive shortcomings in our own efforts by saying "Well, it's better than Maxwell's!"

In the past 20 years alone cameras and equipment have become more sophisticated—and the more sophisticated features more affordable to the hobbyist—than had been the case during the whole half-century or so prior to that. Technical advancements have freed our minds from most of the mechanical details of creating a latent image in a film emulsion, which allows us to concentrate on the esthetics of the situation. Merely recording the image of an animal in reasonable detail is no longer the goal. Wildlife photography has passed out of the novelty stage and, we believe, into the realms of art.

Photography in itself, regardless of subject matter, is a controversial art form. The rarified world of "art" has been very slow to accept a picture created through the mechanical medium of a camera as "valid," when compared to a picture created with brushes or pencils, modeled in wax or carved out of marble. The authors regard this, to put it as gently as possible, as rubbish. The word "snobbery" springs to mind.

Consider what a wildlife photographer does. He selects an instant in the animal's life to record, and he frames this moment in a balanced, dynamic composition, using light as his medium. He is bound by stricter disciplines than any painter, since he cannot direct the animal to move or pose but must accept what nature offers and mould it into a striking picture. It is true that not every wildlife photo is art, since the photographer has an infinity of instants from which to select, but neither is every drawing or painting "art." It is true that his work can be mechanically duplicated, but so can that of a sculptor in bronze or that of a watercolorist. There is still only one original, the work of the artist's eye, hand, and mind. If anything, the wildlife photographer-artist must bring to his work more knowledge and more different kinds of skills and talents than any painter. Jerry Smith is a trained artist and an expert on fine art, as well as a dealer in paintings and prints. How is his eye less discriminating or his taste less refined when he places it behind the viewfinder of a camera? Without belaboring the point, the two of us find the

The title of this picture in a limited
edition is "African Generations,"
because it shows the old cow
elephant accompanied by calves of
different ages, including a daughter
who has a calf of her own. It tells a
story of family closeness unique
among wild animals.
(Photo by John Wootters)

tendency to peer down the art critic's aristocratic nose at photography as an art form both preposterous and arrogant.

As in any other kind of art, wildlife photography has no rigid standards. A good wildlife picture can be needle-sharp or surrealistically blurred, realistic or totally stylized. If it was *intended* to be sharply-focused, however, it must be *sharp;* sloppy focusing cannot pass for creative license. Mechanical mastery of the equipment is a *sine qua non.* On the other hand, gimmickry for its own sake is not great wildlife photography, either. A good photograph makes some kind of statement about the subject and his world, but "See my cute, multiple-image prism filter!" is hardly a valid statement in our opinion. An intentionally blurred photograph of a streaking cheetah can

Author Smith moves in close with a short telephoto lens to record a Texas nighthawk which relies on its camouflage to go unnoticed. Such animals can often be approached surprisingly closely if no sudden moves are made.
(Photo by Mike Alebis)

A striking repetition of forms or patterns can often set a wildlife picture apart, as in the case of these endangered scimitar-horned oryx, originally from the Arabian desert but now extinct in the wild and photographed in the Texas Hill Country, where they thrive.
(Photo by John Wootters)

convey the awesome physical abilities of such a creature with more impact than a "frozen" stop-action shot, but it will come off in that way only when executed with a certain precision, and, intentionally.

Judging wildlife photographs, therefore, becomes an intensely subjective process. The photographer himself is the only person who can fully judge the success of a picture in terms of what he had intended that it be and say. Elsewhere in this book we will discuss how a magazine editor or art director will judge such photos, but a picture which is demonstrably successful in the eyes of the taker may not be worth a dime in the commercial market. Some of the authors' personal favorites among our work have been commercial flops, but they are still favorites of ours. World-acclaimed wildlife painters and sculptors have the same experience.

We will not presume, therefore, to instruct you in judging your own pictures. If you, being as objective as possible about technical considerations, like 'em, they're successful. We may, however, be able to give a few tips.

For example, if you want a shot to be sharp (and most of us do, most of the time), always focus on the eyeball of the creature, if visible. With good light, there will be a tiny highlight there which can be used as a reference with any sort of focusing screen except a split-image type. If you're stuck with the split-image, use the ground-glass field around the split-image disc in the center.

In checking your results (in transparencies), put a magnifier, preferably of at least 8X, on that portion of the picture and study that little highlight. If it's sharp-edged, the picture can be considered sharp, even though the shallow depth-of-field of a telephoto lens may have softened some other parts of the body. If the highlight is round, but fuzzy or diffused, you missed the focus. If it's oval, the picture has either subject movement or camera movement (most likely the latter) in the image.

Focusing on the eye accomplishes several things. First, it's pleasing to a viewer to have the animal's head and face in focus, even if some other parts of its anatomy aren't. Second, it spares the photographer the split-seconds lost in trying to find some other suitably hard-edged part of the subject on which to zero in. And, third, it almost automatically places most creatures' heads near the center of the frame, which, in turn, automatically positions the bulk of the body to one side, or above or below center.

This agrees with the so-called Rule of Thirds, a rule of composition for any square or rectangular scene which has been taught to art students since the Middle Ages. Imagine a standard rectangle divided both horizontally and vertically into equal thirds with two lines drawn each way. These dividing lines will, obviously, intersect at four places in the picture, and orthodox compositional thinking holds that when the center of interest is

A picture which tells the viewer something about the nature of an animal's daily life and how he deals with it is usually more interesting than a mere portrait. This simple but charming shot of a cottontail removing a grassburr from its paw is a perfect example.
(Photo by Jerry Smith)

Here Jerry Smith demonstrates the use of the long bones of arms and legs to support and steady a long lens. The shoulder-stock adds considerable extra steadiness, as well. (Photo by Mike Alebis)

A poignant picture of the nest of a barn owl; the eggs have not yet hatched, but already the mother's instinct to feed her young has caused her to bring a dead rat to the nest. (Photo by Jerry Smith)

The water droplets slashing from the bill of this redhead drake convey the "frozen moment" feeling of being able to look into an instant in nature which the eye could not capture if unaided by the camera. Many outstanding wildlife photographs have this appeal, but it is seldom recognized. (Photo by Jerry Smith)

placed at one of these four points of intersection, the result will be more dynamic and more interesting. I (Wootters) believe that my co-author is almost constitutionally incapable of spotting an animal's body in the center of his field! Working with black-and-white more than he does, I find myself relying on my ability to crop and recompose the shot during the enlargement process, but color transparencies offer most of us considerably less latitude and Jerry Smith's habit is a good one to form.

It should be noted that Smith prefers to work with a plain ground-glass focusing screen with neither microprism nor split-image device. Most of us, on the contrary, rely on some sort of device in the center of the field for focusing, and there is a tendency to shoot when the subject comes up sharp. To do otherwise means that we must focus and then shift the camera slightly to compose; Jerry can focus *and* compose simultaneously anywhere in the field . . . which is the reason for his choice of focusing screens.

If the scene before the lens is dynamic, if there is actual movement or a forceful sense of direction suggested (as by the subject's looking to one side), that movement should always be *into* the frame, rather than out of it. In the case of a creature running or flying at right angles to the axis of the lens, then, the photographer should "lead" it a little, leaving some empty space in front of its nose. The result is invariably much more satisfying to the viewer than the same image with the animal's nose hard up against the edge of the frame.

We suppose that it goes without saying that the horizon (or any other horizontal element) should never be allowed to divide the frame exactly in half, and that the same applies to any strong vertical in the picture.

These things are basic. They are very rarely violated successfully, but they're certainly not rigid rules. A wildlife photographer has a lot on his mind at the moment he snaps a picture. He's thinking of focus, exposure, light angle, and what the subject is most likely to do next, among other things. We do not expound these compositional rules as additional distractions at the moment of shutter release, but as elements to look for when judging and comparing a batch of slides or prints. Gradually, they will become an unconscious habit, built into the cameraman's all-important "eye."

Other than complete mastery of the camera's controls, the greatest thing a wildlife photographer can possess is a fine sense of timing. It is the quality which consistently permits him to pick the precisely-correct instant to expose his film. It allows him to nail the peak of the action, or the subtle cockings of the head or ears by which many creatures communicate their moods and emotions. It cannot, as far as we know, be taught. Some photographers have it, and some never seem to be able to develop that sense of timing to its keenest edge. It's interesting to accompany two expert

The compelling element of this photograph of a coyote is the eyes, the eyes of the hunter, the natural killer. He is not a "nice, wild doggie;" he is a predator, and his eyes show it.
(Photo by Jerry Smith)

The wildlife photographer has the opportunity to make a species like the desperately endangered whooping crane a living creature to his viewers, instead of just a name in a book. Only he can make people who will never see a living crane understand the majesty of these great birds.
(Photo by Jerry Smith)

15

photographers in the field and listen to their shutters when they're working with the identical subject. In action sequences, those two shutters will sound almost as if they were mechanically synchronized. In more static situations, they will click at different times, and close observation will reveal to the observer just what interests each photographer most about the creature. In such situations, two different, equally skilled photographers, working with the same animal at the same time with the same lighting, will get surprisingly different records of the event. And if one of them has that sense of timing we mentioned and the other lacks it, the first may secure a group of pictures which fairly sparkles with the subject's personality while the second produces a series, perhaps just as well-exposed and sharp, which somehow seems a trifle dull and colorless. The difference is really no more than a few tenths of seconds difference in the two photographers' timing.

Whether the innate sense of timing can be developed and honed or not, the mechanics of the problem can be. Every rifleman understands that there is an appreciable time-lag between the microsecond in which his brain says "Fire!" and when the bullet starts to move. The nerve impulses take time to travel to the muscles of his trigger finger, the muscles take time to contract, and the machinery takes time to function. Exactly the same time-lag occurs in photography. Hyperprecise laboratory equipment can very easily measure the lapse of time between the cameraman's decision to take the picture and the actual opening and closing of the shutter, and this time-lag is noticeably longer with a single-lens reflex camera, where the mirror must move out of the way, than with a leaf-shutter.

This means that the photographer must actually "lead" the action he wishes to record slightly, or, to put it another way, he must begin the process of taking a picture of a certain action *before* that action begins to occur. He must, therefore, be alert and exceptionally sensitive to what is about to happen to time his shots properly. And, no, he cannot simply mash the button and rely on a fast motor drive to catch the instant he desires! Beginners never believe that statement; but they'll quickly learn the truth of it in the field.

In addition to a sufficiently thorough understanding of the nature of the beast before the lens to make accurate, instantaneous decisions about what he'll do next, the wildlife photographer needs an intuitive knowledge of his own time-lag, using that particular camera. This is a "feel" that will come in time, but that time can probably be shortened somewhat by simple practice. One possible way to set up such practice, for example, is in the backyard in which garden birds are coming to a feeder.

You will notice, if you watch, that they have certain favorite "staging-up"

*If a sculptor was seeking
a reference photograph which
conveyed the noble bearing,
masculinity, and alertness of
a great whitetail buck, he
couldn't do better than this one!
(Photo by Jerry Smith)*

Small reptiles like this green anole are a neglected and interesting source of subjects for the amateur wildlife photographer, and can be found almost everywhere. (Photo by Jerry Smith)

The eye-spots on the inner wings of this moth are supposed to frighten away predators, but the textures in this scene were what fascinated the photographer. (Photo by John Wootters)

18

places, specific limbs or twigs where each bird waits his turn to swoop to the feeder. In this situation, the photographer knows where the bird will start from and where he's going. Place yourself at right angles to that line of flight and focus on its midpoint, and then try to nail each bird just as his trajectory passes a certain element of the background, perhaps a tree trunk or the corner of the garage.

When the pictures are developed, you will almost certainly notice that, if you thought you snapped the shutter *exactly* as the bird passed the reference mark, his image on the film will be well *past* that mark, every time. How far past it the subject got before the frame was exposed would, if the bird's speed were known, allow a fairly accurate calculation of the photographer's time-lag with that camera, but that's not what's important. What is important is his intuitive perception of the time-lag, and his ability to allow for it in future exercises of the same sort. When subsequent photos in the same situation reveal the images of the swooping birds more or less exactly coincident with that background reference mark, the photographer has perfected his timing, at least in the physiomechanical sense.

Backgrounds make or break a surprising number of wildlife photographs. Newcomers frequently complain that they're stuck with the background, having no control over where the subject wildlife chooses to be, and claim the image of the animal is the important thing. We feel that the *picture* is the important thing, and the picture is a product of all the elements present, especially including the background. Furthermore, we have more control over where the subject chooses to place himself than may be apparent at first glance; this will be the subject of a couple of chapters later on in this book. In some cases, where the photographer plans to wait in ambush for his subjects, as at a waterhole or feeding station, he can place himself so that a desirable background will appear behind his expected wild visitors.

Finally, a long telephoto lens tends to pull objects out of the background via their inherently shallow field of sharp focus, often reducing the background to a sort of textured blur against which the creature stands out sharply. The larger the aperture, of course, the shallower the zone of sharpness and the more completely the background will be nullified as a detailed element in the composition. Many of the newer, faster telephotos are perfectly sharp wide-open, but the less expensive or older lenses tend to reach maximum sharpness a stop or two from maximum. With this in mind, a background conscious photographer can add dimension and delineation to his subject by choosing to shoot at the widest *sharp* setting on his lens, adjusting his shutter speed as necessary to control exposure. With the slower lenses and film emulsions, it usually works out this way as a matter of course. Where there is enough light to give the cameraman a

Her kitten is playing happily, but this mother bobcat is none too happy at the intrusion of the photographer, and it shows in her eyes. (Photo by Jerry Smith)

19

Although little anatomical detail of this American alligator is shown here, the picture conveys the sinister, saurian personality of the creature as it really is. (Photo by Jerry Smith)

choice, it still may be best to shoot with the lens at maximum aperture, to set the subject apart from the background. Many species tend to blend with their environment in color and often in shape and markings as well, and can actually be seen better in a photo with a deliberately shallow depth-of-field than by the deep-focus human eye in habitat. The important thing is that the photographer be thinking of his backgrounds and their effects in his finished pictures with every shot, and doing what he can to make them favorable to the effect he desires.

What goes into a great wildlife picture? We would list diligence, patience, knowledge of the wildlife, and imagination as the paramount qualities a wildlife photographer must bring to his art. This kind of photography is, like most art forms, about nine parts discipline and determination and one part luck, inspiration, and technical mastery of the medium.

All these things contribute to placing the photographer with his camera within range of the subject and to sharp, well-exposed, well-framed pictures. But there is more to a great picture than merely an image from which the species can be readily identified. For lack of a better term, let's call it "excitement," an impact on the emotions of the viewer. It is that elusive quality which somehow expresses the "wolfness" of a wolf, if you will, and sets him before the onlooker not merely as a specimen of his species but as an individual living creature with a distinctive personality and set of opinions, needs, motivations, and reactions, integrated and interacting with all the other ecological components of his habitat, including mankind. Imagine a picture of a mother owl arriving at her nest with a rat in her talons. It can express her fierceness as a predator as contrasted with her concern for her babies. It can evoke a response on behalf of the powerful mother owl, the helpless babies, or the dead rat . . . or all three. It says something about the owl's niche in the ecology, and perhaps something about her future in this parlous world. It may or may not direct the viewer's response (every viewer puts as much into any picture as he gets out of it), but it demands some kind of response.

That is the "something extra," the excitement, in a great wildlife photograph. It is not a product of chance or expensive lenses or darkroom magic. It is the product of a human mind, a discerning eye behind the viewfinder, and imagination. We believe that these qualities cannot be taught, only recognized and admired when they appear. Pictures which reveal them transcend mere "wildlife photography," and even "photography" as a medium, and become pure art. They interpret our world for us.

They are exceedingly rare. They are also worth striving for, and the equipment and techniques available to that end are the subject of the remainder of this book.

2

Tools Of The Trade: Cameras And Lenses

Because of the differences in background and professional requirements pointed out in the Preface, this chapter and the next will be written by the co-authors separately. We have pointed out the differences, but they are merely differences in the answers each of us has chosen to the common problems. It may be well to insert a word or two here in definition of those problems.

Wildlife photography is very rarely performed under ideal conditions. We deal with shy and skittish creatures who do not trust humans, and many of whom are nocturnal. We have little or no control over light, and often have our best chances very early or very late in the day. We may have to travel by horseback, boat, or four-wheel-drive vehicle, but most commonly afoot, and we may climb mountains, wade swamps, dive into the sea in search of our subjects.

All this adds up to pretty severe demands upon our equipment. It must be reasonably lightweight and compact, fast to bring into action and flexible, and as durable as possible in the face of dust, dew, and hard knocks. We need long lenses and fast lenses, preferably in the *same* lense.

The perfect camera for this work, of course, has yet to be invented, but the modern single-lens-reflex (SLR) of good quality in 35 mm format comes closer than anything else. Author Smith has no trouble getting 20x24 inches (and often much larger) salon-grade prints from 35 mm Kodachrome 64 slides, and every editor and art director in North America will not only accept but may actually prefer good 35 mms to any larger format. Incredibly fast, long-focal-length lenses are available which, with the faster films, permit the wildlife photographer to hand-hold shots at high

To capture the flight of a bumblebee from flower to flower demands the right equipment and a keen sense of timing. (Photo by Mike Alebis)

Jerry Smith favors the Nikon system but has added the Leitz Teleyt 400mm and the Questar 700mm for specialized wildlife photography purposes. (Photo by Jerry Smith)

The Questar 700mm is of superb quality, but, at an effective aperture of f/11, too slow for wildlife photography except with the fastest films. It is, however, an outstanding "effects" lens. (Photo by Jerry Smith)

shutter speeds in low light levels. Curtain shutters at speeds at 1/2,000th second guarantee stopped action, even at the wingtips of flying birds. And the array of lenses, filters, winders, drives, dedicated strobes, and other accessories available for all of the better "system" cameras on the market today make the basic body into the most versatile photographic instrument in history.

This is not to say that if you already have a good 2¼ x 2¼ format camera (SLR or even one of the twin-lens models with lens interchangeability), you cannot take wildlife pictures. You can, but you will carry more weight and bulk, spend more money, change film more often, and take fewer photos. With ingenuity, patience, and an understanding of your subjects, nearly anything can be made to produce the occasional wildlife picture; author Wootters took his first ones with a fixed-focus, fixed-exposure, 620 Box Brownie, during the 1940s and '50s, and won prizes in several photo contests with them. More recently, he has pressed the new Pentax Auto 110 system into emergency service now and then with acceptable results. However, to attempt any halfway-serious wildlife photography with anything less suitable than a good 35 mm SLR is very likely to be a waste of time, in our opinion.

With that brief discussion as background, the following remarks, produced individually by the co-authors can be interpreted. First, Jerry Smith:

* * *

Since I was one of the first photographers in my area to become interested in wildlife, and especially big game animals, I had nobody else with whom to compare notes and results. I shot a lot of rolls of film with an amateur camera rig and was reasonably well satisfied with my results, because I didn't know any better. When I finally got a chance to see some slides produced by a professional, I realized that I was looking at some really sharp images for the first time. I also knew at once that I was going to have to get some better equipment, regardless of cost.

That was alright with me; my old camera was about worn out (it was secondhand when I acquired it) and, like all photographers, I had a craving for a new one, anyway.

The Nikon F-2 had just been introduced and seemed to fit all my requirements. It had interchangeable focusing screens, a center-weighted through-the-lens (TTL) light meter, a bayonet lens mount, and a motor drive.

A motor drive! Visions of machinegun-style shooting ran through my head. With a motor drive, no shot would be out of my grasp! Anything was possible. I felt invincible. I just couldn't wait to get my hands on the new camera with motor drive.

*A very long lens like the Questar
700mm can produce outstanding
special effects when the
photographer takes advantage of
the perspective-compression
inherent in such instruments. Here,
the foreshortening effect of
the Questar is used to exaggerate
the size of the setting sun's disc
as a backdrop for a flock
of roosting mourning doves.
(Photo by Jerry Smith)*

When I did, I found them to be everything I'd hoped for . . . but I also found out that it was still quite possible for me to miss a shot, even with the miraculous motor drive. Furthermore, I discovered that I did not and could not use the motor drive in the field as I had envisioned it. On moving animals, it just wasn't possible to keep a sharp focus on my subject with that drive running at full speed.

Nowadays, I'd hate to have to do without the motor drive, but it's a convenience, not a necessity. I find I seldom fire more than two shots in sequence. The advantage, of course, is that it's faster and less distracting not to have to thumb-crank that lever after every shot, and I never miss a chance because I forgot to advance the film and cock the shutter.

At the same time I ordered the F-2 and drive, I decided I couldn't live without a 400 mm Leitz Teleyt. It featured slide focusing and came with a collapsible shoulder stock. Lenses of this caliber, I quickly found out, are not readily available from your friendly neighborhood camera shop. Many phone calls later, I located a used 400 mm Teleyt in New York, and sent for it. To this day it is still my favorite wildlife lens, even though it is slow, bulky, and not easy to get a critical focus quickly. After "dry-firing" my new camera and lens for about a day to get used to the controls, I took my first two rolls of film. The results were astounding to me. For the first time in my own work, I saw *sharp* images! Eyes, bodies, and tails. I knew then how it feels to get really outstanding results.

My next lens purchase was a 200 mm f / 4 Nikkor, which I used for a short time and soon abandoned for a 180 mm f / 2.8, another Nikon lens. The 180 mm is not only faster but much sharper than the 200 mm, and is usually the first lens used when starting an early morning photography trip, because of its speed.

Another lens I thought I just had to have but which has been a disappointment is my 700 mm Questar, a so-called "mirror" lens. It was advertised as a wildlife photographer's lens and was claimed to be hand-holdable. I can tell you that if you use Kodachrome 64 film, it is *not* hand-holdable, and is almost impossible to use even with a sandbag rest. The lens has a specified, fixed f-stop of f / 8, but I find it to be, effectively, on f / 11, at best, which means your shutter speed with K64 will be around 1 / 30th second most of the time, given good light. With fast film and a sturdy tripod, the Questar may have some applications in wildlife photography but for the average photographer doing my kind of picture taking, it's simply out of the question. I still have it, but use it rarely, and then only as a special effects lens when I want the perspective compression of a super telephoto. An example might be an animal in the foregound silhouetted against a giant orange ball of a setting sun.

All mirror lenses produce fairly sharp images in the center of the field but usually have some "vignetting" around the edges. They also produce unusual, doughnut-shaped highlights which may be okay in some kinds of commercial photography but look unnatural to me in wildlife scenes. I do not recommend them as general purpose wildlife lenses, in any focal length.

Since my entry into serious photography in 1972, there have been some tremendous improvements in telephoto lens quality. This new generation of lenses offers such things as internal focusing, in which the rear lens group moves *inside* the lens barrel as the focusing ring is turned, and the overall length of the instrument does not change. Focusing is almost effortless, and very minute adjustments in focus are easy. One of the problems I've encountered with my old favorite Leitz 400 mm is that its "trombone-style" slide focusing may require passing the critical point two or three times on a stationary subject before the right spot is found. While I'm doing all this, I may have lost my subject. The Leitz sliding focus system, however, is very quick and smooth for follow-focusing on a fast-moving subject.

After wasting two whole days in a row while trying to get shots of a trophy whitetail buck and failing because of poor lighting, I made up my mind to try one of the new, super-fast, internal focus lenses. The one I chose is the new Nikon IF ED 400 mm f/3.5. Again, I had the problem of trying to find an expensive, specialty lens of this kind for sale, but my camera shop located one in Chicago and had it airfreighted to me. It arrived right in the middle of the whitetail deer rutting season, and I put it immediately to work.

This is an impressive piece of glassware. It has a huge front element that looks like the eye of a giant cyclops, being five inches across at the front and slightly more than 12 inches in length. It weighs quite a lot and is very front-heavy. It has a nonreflective, black "crackle" finish and requires little or no extra camouflaging for wildlife use. Nikon claims this lens to be "the fastest 400 mm lens on the market today, and one of the sharpest and easiest to use." My trials of it have engendered a great respect for it in actual use . . . but nothing's perfect, as I'll point out below.

This lens is indeed extremely sharp, even when wide-open (f/3.5).Turning the focusing ring reminded me of the first time I ever felt the luxury of a real suede coat. I find myself playing with it, just to enjoy its silky smoothness. Actual focusing is virtually a snap! You are either in focus or out; there's no "in-between."

Since I seldom use a tripod, I fitted the new 400 mm to a shoulder stock, with an F-2 body and motor drive attached. The considerable weight of the whole rig is both a boon and a bother. As an experienced competition pistol and rifle shooter, I know that a heavy—and especially a muzzle-heavy—gun is easier to hold steady, at least for short periods. The same is true of long

This leopard frog on a log happens to be author Smith's very first effort at wildlife photography. (Photo by Jerry Smith)

Jerry Smith's favorite rig for low-light, low-contrast situations features the new Nikon ED f/3.5 400mm lens shown here. In normal-contrast lighting with Kodachrome 64 film, however, this super telephoto is almost too contrasty, often blocking up shadows and washing out highlights. (Photo by Jerry Smith)

camera lenses. The weight tends to damp out minor muscular tremors. This Nikon f/3.5 seems steady as a rock in the sitting or even in the standing position, but it's just impossible to keep it in shooting position for any length of time without resting.

For shooting from a blind, using a tripod, or for an experienced outdoorsman in good physical condition, the extra weight of such lenses is no great problem, although if much walking or climbing is on the schedule it might require a second thought. In any case, it's something to be considered before buying any long lens.

As to picture quality with this lens: it's superb in low light situations—a cloudy day or before sunrise, or anytime natural light contrast is low. Such difficult conditions are common in wildlife photography, and are the reason I invested in this very expensive piece of glass in the first place. It is inherently an extremely high-contrast lens, so high, in fact, that it doesn't work so well in normally lighted scenes with shadow areas. The shadows tend to block up and lose detail while the hard highlights may wash out entirely, at least when using a high-contrast film like K64. With lower-contrast films such as the Ektachromes or Kodacolors, the problem would be lessened.

My original intention had been to sell the old, much slower Leitz 400 mm if I was satisfied with the new Nikon ED. With some field experience with both, however, I have chosen to keep both in my battery, using the Nikon early and late in the day and under cloudy conditions and changing to the Leitz for high-contrast, brightly sunlit photographs.

That's the best of both worlds, which my livelihood permits me to enjoy. If forced by economics to keep only one of these great lenses, it would be the old Leitz through which have been exposed so many slides which eventually became magazine covers, centerspreads, and limited editions. It may not be perfect, either . . . but, as I said, nothing is, at least in wildlife photography equipment.

* * *

The above were the words of Jerry Smith. Now, on the same subjects, comes John Wootters, in testimony whereof he witnesseth:

* * *

Although not without experience with Leica, Contax, and Nikon products, I use the Canon system. My first Canon camera was acquired while I was in the Army and stationed in Korea during the early 1950s and it was a Japanese copy of the then-current Leica III-C rangefinder model. During the next two decades, I acquired each new Canon model, and, when the F-1 was introduced about 1970, I traded everything in and started over.

At that time, I would have as readily converted to the Nikon system, except that the Canon F-1 offered several advantages not possessed by

Sometimes a very small element in a wildlife photograph can set it apart. In this case, the buck's tongue, licking his nose, is that element. (Photo by Jerry Smith)

Particularly with insects, sheer mass of numbers can make an interesting shot, as in the case of this swarm of wild honeybees. (Photo by Jerry Smith)

The equipment author Wootters uses for wildlife photography is based on the Canon F-1 system, but includes lenses from Soligor and Vivitar. The shorter lens shown are, from left, a 28mm wide-angle, 100mm telephoto (f/2.8), and 50mm Macro. (Photo by John Wootters)

the Nikon F (but since incorporated into subsequent models) such as total interchangeability between bodies of the motor drive and a built-in through-the-lens spot metering system. My own resolution tests showed the Canon lenses, overall, to be at least the equal of the Nikon lenses in sharpness and contrast.

Since then, the Nikon people have more than kept pace in technology, especially in motor drives, and at this moment I would see little to choose from between the two systems (except for price); like most of us, however, I now have such an investment in lenses and accessories that switching systems at this point would be an economic backbreaker.

For wildlife purposes, as was mentioned in the beginning, a 35 mm SLR system is the only kind with sufficient flexibility and portability which is consistently capable of producing the quality required by editors. Since the "professional" and "amateur" models in each manufacturer's line mostly use the same lenses, any differences must be in the bodies. For the most part, a professional 35 mm camera body is manufactured to somewhat higher standards of durability. Shutter speeds, for example, will remain more or less nominal despite the gear-train wear inflicted by a professional photographer who may shoot several hundred pictures almost every day for years.

The camera body and all incident machinery must stand up to such environmental hazards as dust, moisture, and salt air, as well as the inevitable hard knocks outdoor usage entails. All these things are part of the serious wildlife photographer's working conditions, too, suggesting that he will be well off to spring for the professional model, even if he has to grunt when he writes the check.

Another point I find important is the interchangeable focusing screen, a feature found mostly in the professional camera bodies. The reason is the fact that the wildlife photographer so frequently uses telephoto lenses, usually of a rather small maximum aperture. I like a microprism focusing screen, but the same such screen will not work equally well with an f/1.4 normal lens and an f/4.5 or 5.6 telephoto. Interchangeability allows me to keep one of my F-1 bodies equipped with a screen especially designed for lenses with small maximum apertures and the others set up for standard lenses.

The combination screen which so often comes standard today with new cameras, the one with a small split-image "spot" in the center, surrounded by a narrow microprism ring, surrounded by plain ground-glass, is the work of the devil, as far as I'm concerned, and useful for absolutely nothing! In a system without interchangeability of screens, you're stuck with it.

Metering is critical in wildlife photography, where we deal so often with marginal light conditions or with subjects in heavy shadow within an otherwise brightly lit scene. The necessity to work rapidly when we actually catch up with the beast we're trying to record almost mandates a reliable through-the-lens (TTL) metering system. It's true that a photographer who sticks exclusively to only one type of film long enough can develop an excellent eye for exposure conditions . . . but, oh! the frustrations he'll suffer until he achieves that elusive skill! For me, the Canon F-1's spot-metering system is the perfect solution, most especially when using long lenses. Only a small rectangle in the center of the field is being metered, and the longer the lens, the smaller the actual area measured. This lets me meter the body of a deer standing in heavy shadow if necessary, or to average the reading for the whole field with a quick horizontal or vertical swing.

Those systems in which the whole field is metered and averaged, whether center-weighted, foreground-weighted, or whatever, perform well, but routinely require the photographer to exercise a little judgment, under or overexposing the meter's instructions a half-stop or full-stop on almost every wildlife shot. If the Canon system did not include spot metering, I suspect I'd invest in a hand-held spot meter.

How about automatic exposure setting? It has its uses, but I would consider it only in a camera which offers the photographer his choice of aperture priority, shutter speed priority, *and* manual override. All three modes are required in wildlife photography. If forced to a choice, I'd pick shutter speed priority, but few of the newer cameras with only one option are set up in this mode.

Overall, I must add that I know no professional wildlife photographers who routinely use any automatic exposure setting system, and have no use for it myself. When I occasionally use my wife's Canon A-1, I always set it in manual mode, thus losing the use of several hundred dollars' worth of sophisticated electronics. Automatic exposure works beautifully when the subject is front-lighted in a scene of fairly uniform illumination and normal contrast range, but, unfortunately, hardly one out of a hundred wildlife opportunities occur in such utopian circumstances.

The 1/2,000th-second shutter speed available in many high-quality cameras may be a good selling point but is seldom used in the field. With most films of ASA ratings up to 100, there's never enough light even for 1/1,000th, and rarely for a 500th, for that matter. Long (and slow) lenses complicate the problem. We do need action-stopping capability, but it's usually limited by necessary compromises. If and when faster color films with the desirable characteristics of the Kodachromes come onto the market, the higher shutter speed settings will become more and more useful.

An opossum is a slow, lugubrious animal of the night, a living antique that survives by the ultimate in passive resistance— feigning death. The photographer rarely has a daytime opportunity like this on these marsupials. (Photo by John Wootters)

As a sidelight, my co-author is an example of the adaptive skills developed by an expert photographer around the technical limitations of equipment and materials. Because he uses what I consider a slow (ASA 64) film and, mostly, slow lenses and thus finds himself working with a relatively slow shutter speed most of the time, he has mastered to an unbelievable degree the knack of panning through fast-action, producing pictures of a deer exploding into flight, for example, with the eye and head razor sharp and the body reasonably so, with blurring in the legs and background which imparts a strong sense of movement. I know of no other cameraman in the world who can do this as well as Jerry.

I suspect, too, that his choices of gear and films have actually moulded his tastes to some degree, as well, since he is not pleased by action photos which are "frozen" by a high shutter speed.

As to lenses, and speaking strictly from the wildlife photographer's point of view, I would advise the following: a mild (28 mm to 35 mm) wide-angle; the 50 mm fast normal lens; a macro (ideally 100 mm); a mild telephoto in the range of 85 mm to 135 mm; and a long telephoto of 300 mm or, preferably, 400 mm. Beginning at the long end of this spectrum, I am convinced that 400 mm is the ideal, all-purpose focal length for wildlife,

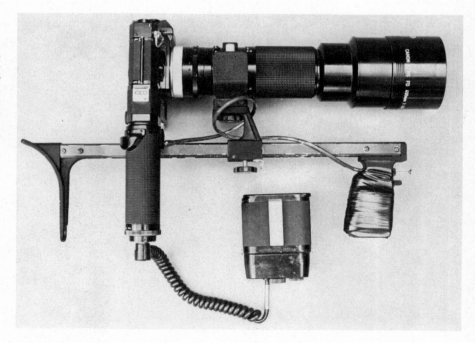

Author Wootters' standard wildlife-photography rig features this excellent but unmarked shoulder stock, the first model of Canon motor drives for the F-1 system with separate battery pack, and the Canon f/4.5 400mm SSC lens. (Photo by John Wootters)

37

Although done mostly in the outdoors, wildife photography offers many situations in which use of a strobe fill-in can make or break the shot. On this nesting mourning dove with her squabs, it made it. (Photo by Jerry Smith)

Sticking with the same camera system means total, instinctive familiarity with the controls, vital in fast-action situations like this shot at a running javelina, or collared peccary. (Photo by Mike Alebis)

offering the best available compromises between image size, lens speed, and ease of hand-holding at modest shutter speeds. Lenses longer than 400 mm almost demand a tripod, are mostly useful only in fairly specialized circumstances to begin with, and the longer the focal length, the more true all these comments become.

Lenses of 250 to 300 mm are usually not much, if any, faster than 400s and result in a smaller image on the negative.

The moderate telephoto I mentioned (mine is a fast 100 mm) has all sorts of uses, not the least of which is as a macro when used with a bellows or extension tubes for studio work. It's also excellent for species which can be approached fairly closely, giving less critical focusing for dim light and fast-action work. In Africa, I have found it all I needed for big animals in game parks (elephants, for instance) and good for herd shots. It's also a neat portrait lens.

The 100 mm macro mentioned is for the insects, tiny reptiles and amphibians, and as an "effects" lens. A 50 mm macro with a short extension tube can provide a larger image (up to 1-to-1), but must be placed so close to the subject that it's nearly impossible to light it properly. The 100 mm macro gives a little elbow room for lighting the subject, especially important when said subject isn't inclined to stay put but insists on wiggling, crawling, or creeping away.

The major utilization for a normal lens in wildlife photography is with a flash for night shots, where the great speed in most modern lenses extends the distance to which the strobe offers adequate illumination. Of course, it's the lens that comes with the camera and it does have other uses (we assume even the most diehard wildlife photographer occasionally pops a shot or two of his or her children).

A moderate wide-angle lens is of limited utility for animals, but has its uses in the cramped quarters of some zoos, for flushing-bird shots, and, now and then, for a panorama with a single animal or a herd in the foreground. Its chief virtue for my purposes is the exceptional depth-of-field, and one not shorter than 35 mm can assure sharp focus in many situations at close range where not enough light for visual focusing is present.

There are other kinds of lenses. Like all professionals, I am often asked about "zooms," or variable focal length lenses. Like most professionals, I'm suspicious of them, while acknowledging their advantages. I find them more satisfactory in the shorter ranges, typically 35 mm to 85 mm, or 70 mm to 210 mm, and do not use them in the longer ranges. In photography as in most other aspects of life, you do not get something for nothing, and for the flexibility in framing of a zoom lens you must expect to give something up, usually lens speed and light weight, if nothing else. Many lack a

Author Smith feels the wild turkey is one of the most difficult of all species of American wildlife to expose correctly, because of the extreme contrast and iridescence of his plumage. A cloudy-bright day helped him succeed with this wild gobbler. (Photo by Jerry Smith)

Panning on a running animal like this peccary with a relatively slow shutter-speed can produce a great sense of motion and speed, and produce a striking photo when the subject's head and eye is sharp. Not easy, but always worth trying for! (Photo by Jerry Smith)

The pyrrhuloxia is an uncommon bird of the arid southwest. This is a young male. (Photo by Jerry Smith)

truly flat field and some lack that ultimate sharpness which for the wildlife cameraman is worth much fine gold. I would not purchase a zoom without testing it very thoroughly with my own equipment.

I will admit, however, that I possess and find very useful a Vivitar Series 1 70 to 210 mm variable with a macro feature. Although I rarely point it at a wild animal while set to its longer length, there have been times when I was glad it would extend to 210 mm.

Another question regularly asked concerns the catadioptric, or "mirror" lenses. Their principal appeal comes from their remarkably light weight and compact size in relation to focal length, and these are important features for wildlife. Commonly cited drawbacks are lack of speed and the now-famous little doughnut-shaped highlights. A personal objection is harder to define, but it is simply that a mirror does some infinitely subtle but unpleasant things to the background, resulting in photographic effects which do not please me. With a more or less uniform, featureless background (like sky), however, this objection disappears. I have a Canon 500 mm mirror lens which is said to be an $f/8$ and is actually an $f/11$, but use it sparingly. It will do some things that none of my other glassware will, but it is definitely not an all-around, standard wildlife lens.

Another question concerns the so-called "follow-focus" lens, of which the best known is the Novoflex. These have squeeze-type pistol grips to change focus and are very fast and smooth, particularly in taking pictures of flying birds. The ones I've tried are quite sharp in the center of the field but noticeably softer near the edges, which eliminates them in my eyes as general purpose instruments.

My standard wildlife lens is the Canon 400 mm SSC $f/4.5$, and I consider it the best lens for the purpose in the world, for the money. At a retail list price of about $1,000 as this is written (you can usually buy one for something under $800), it isn't cheap, but it's a steal in comparison to the special glass or flourite lenses which are the only ones to beat it in speed, contrast, and sharpness; *they* cost from $2,500 to $3,500 in similar focal lengths! They are also tremendously heavy and bulky.

On the other hand, the 400 mm SSC really is much better than the "brand-X" 400s of the $250 price category as its cost would suggest, being sharp when wide-open (which is where a wildlife lens stays most of the time) and featuring a rear-group, variable-cam focusing mechanism which is fast and sure.

After a good selection of lenses, the most useful accessory for wildlife is undoubtedly a motor drive (or a winder; the only real difference is speed). With experience, you will find that the fast, sequential shooting capability of a drive is very seldom actually used in the field. The main reason is that it is

This scene reveals one of the relatively rare opportunities to make effective use of filters in wildlife photography. A red filter with Tri-X Pan film produced the dramatic sky effects here. (Photo by John Wootters)

almost impossible to maintain a decent focus on a rapidly moving beast with that mirror flopping up and down several times per second. If the critter happens to be running *across* your front instead of *away,* of course, this is no drawback, and I once did get pictures of a rhinoceros bull charging across a narrow opening in the bush which would have been impossible without the drive at full speed. It is, therefore, nice to have but, in truth, a little-used feature. The great values of a drive are lack of distraction when the action gets fast and lack of hand movements to draw attention to the photographer at any other time. I particularly like the Nikon's power-rewind feature, too, which my Canons lack. Changing film in the presence of an animal is tough and time consuming enough even *with* the power-rewind.

About three shots per second is as fast as I want a motor drive to run. Those with higher speeds are occasionally nice, but I wouldn't pay a dime extra for the extra frames-per-second rate. Actually a simple winder, capable of two frames-per-second, will do most of it quieter and with less weight and bulk.

Next on the list would be an electronic flash unit, or strobe. Two or even three is better, in which case one should be the main, on-camera unit with both automatic and thyristor circuitry features and the other(s) should be

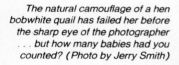

The natural camouflage of a hen bobwhite quail has failed her before the sharp eye of the photographer . . . but how many babies had you counted? (Photo by Jerry Smith)

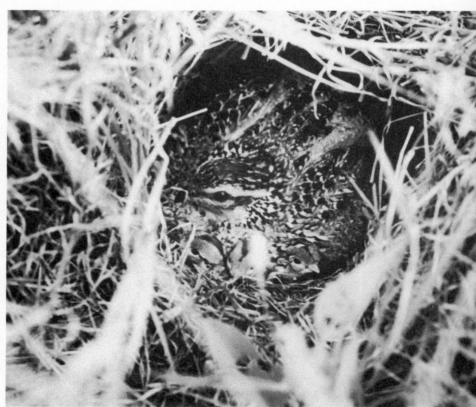

less powerful and can be manual only, and thus cheaper. You'll need one slave unit (with P/C cord, if needed) for each extra unit. I have learned to hate rechargeable, "ni-cad" batteries and refuse to purchase units requiring them. Try recharging them in the middle of Africa or the Yukon sometime! Extra alkaline batteries are easy to carry and can be bought in almost every crossroads filling station, wherever in the world you may find yourself.

One of the most universal of wildlife photography accessories is variously called a shoulder stock, gun stock mount, shoulder-pod, or whatever. Whatever it may be called, I regard it as absolutely essential to photography with a long lens, but I tried a dozen different types over many years before I found one I considered satisfactory. Unfortunately, I do not even know the brand name, but the accompanying photos may help identify it. All the other models I've seen, with the exception of the Leitz version used by Jerry Smith, were too heavy, impossibly awkward to use, or would not take a motor drive-equipped camera. Before I located the one I use today, I had taken some measurements from Jerry's Leitz shoulder-pod and had decided that I could fabricate its equivalent with about five dollars' worth of materials available at my corner hardware store. That sounded like a good idea, since the Letiz sells for several hundred dollars!

The virtues of the Leitz style are that it leaves both the photographer's hands on the camera controls for maximum flexibility and that the hooked buttplate helps support the weight of a long, heavy lens without additional muscular effort. It also adds minimal weight to the rig. It still seems ideal to me, and I may yet get around to constructing one, but the model shown on my own gear works well enough that laziness has so far prevented that project.

The importance of some sort of shoulder support is simply that it will improve your percentage of negatives or slides showing no camera movement by about 50 percent, and the slower the shutter speeds used, the greater the improvement. Another way to put it would be that the shoulder stock will permit you to shoot one shutter speed increment slower than you must ordinarily use to get an acceptable proportion of negatives without camera movement. If you think about it, that's almost like adding one full f-stop to your lens' speed, allowing you to get satisfactory results in about half the light you formerly required. It makes a *big* difference when the game starts moving, as is its wont, just after sunrise and right at dusk.

Before I found my shoulder-pod, I tried a telescoping belt-pod, a sort of short monopod with a clip to hook over the trousers belt. I also tried (and still use, very occasionally and under special circumstances) a monopod, and various devices intended to affix a pan-tilt head to automobile windows,

*The rookeries or roosting colonies
of waterbirds offer consistently
good photographic possibilities.
(Photo by Jerry Smith)*

47

tree limbs, and various other objects. And, of course, a tripod does now and then come in handy.

The trouble with all these gilhickeys was lack of flexibility. You never know where an animal or bird will turn up, or from which direction he'll come, and it will regularly be from the one you least expect. Only a shoulder-pod permits you to turn and twist and train the lens in any direction on short notice without excessive movement of your whole body. Of course, with lenses in excess of about 500 mm focal length, a solid tripod is almost mandated. There's just no way around it.

On the subject of steadiness, incidentally, I've heard it said, often by authorities, that one cannot consistently hand-hold lens over 200 or 300 mm. This is sheer nonsense. Anyone of normal muscular development can *learn* to hand-hold up to 400 mm with a shoulder stock, but the key word there is "learn." It takes practice. The secret is what a trained rifleman calls trigger control, the knack of releasing the shutter without introducing a muscular tremor into the system. This is much more easily learned with the newer cameras with electornic shutter releases than with the older, mechanical style, but it must be *consciously* practiced and perfected with any kind of camera. Being an experienced rifle and handgun shooter before I took up photography, it came naturally to me, and I was interested to note that Jerry Smith, although not a hunter, is also an expert marksman. The standard method of perfecting trigger control for a target shooter is called dry-firing, repeatedly taking aim on a small target with an empty gun and squeezing the trigger off, watching for the slightest movement of the sights against the target. It could well be that a modified version of such practice with an empty camera would be as helpful to the long lens photographer.

How about filters? Most professionals I know consistently keep a "skylight" or ultraviolet filter over their camera lenses, except for the largest ones, just to protect that precious glassware from dust and smudges. They prefer to risk the finish and coating of an $18 filter to that of a $1,000 lens. I own and occasionally use standard yellow and red filters, as well as several kinds of "effects" filters—star, fog, duotone, and others . . . but it must be remembered that I shoot a great deal more black-and-white film than does my co-author, or most other photographers. A photo of mine appears in these pages which illustrates the rather specialized uses of such filters, a picture of a pair of whitetail bucks silhouetted against a spectacular, cloud-filled sky. That sky is the result of a red filter with Eastman Tri-X film.

Some of the other accessory gimmicks I use—such things as photoelectric, infrared, radio-controlled, and mechanical release devices for remote and subject actuated photography—will be mentioned and illustrated in subsequent chapters.

3

Tools Of The Trade: Films And Materials

*E*very wildlife photographer whose work is exhibited is invariably asked what films he uses, and the inquirer usually seems a little disappointed that we use the same films he does. We suppose it's natural for beginners in the field to hope that there are special, professional-grade films available which can explain the difference between his own early efforts and those of a successful wildlife photographer.

Alas, no such luck. Some of the difference may be in equipment, most of it is in how we use the equipment and films, and none of it lies in our access to any kind of secret super film.

The perfect wildlife film is not yet on the market, and when it is introduced, it will be called "Kodachrome 200" (according to author Smith; Wootters is still holding out for "Kodachrome 400!"). This is another way of saying that, at least in color reversal (slide) films, today's Eastman Kodachrome 64 has everything we need except the emulsion speed. It is, for practical purposes, grainless, its color response and rendition is very pleasing, and it is relatively resistant to the effects of heat.

Its slow emulsion speed is a distinct handicap to the wildlife photographer, however. We remember the first day the co-authors spent in the field together, in some of Smith's favorite terrain. Wootters was surprised that we didn't hurry into the deer coverts before sun-up and felt we were missing the best time. Later that afternoon, Smith put away his cameras and chauffeured Wootters around for two more hours, during which he secured pictures which have been published often. Finally, in good natured impatience, Smith remarked, "I don't understand what you're doing, trying to take pictures in the dark!" It was only 5:00 p.m. on an early autumn day.

This rare photo of two big whitetail
bucks fighting was shot on a
cloudy-dull day and was actually a
little underexposed on Kodachrome
64 transparency film. The
compressed tonal values, however,
permitted an excellent conversion
to black-and-white.
(Photo by Jerry Smith)

The difference was that Smith was loaded with Kodachrome 64, while Wootters was shooting black-and-white Tri-X at a nominal rating of ASA 400. Not only was Wootters able to get equivalent exposure values with 2½ stops less light, but he could exercise considerable contrast control during the processing and printing of the resulting negatives. Obviously, an ideal film for wildlife would combine the virtues of both films.

It may be an ideal that is never attained, not because it is a technological impossibility (some special film emulsions manufactured for NASA go far beyond these relatively modest specifications), but because the manufacturer perceives the market as unprofitable and because he doesn't wish to compete with his own high-speed "Process E-6" color slide films, which we know as the Ektachrome family. Of which, more later.

Other than the obvious pictorial qualities—fine-grain, high resolution, and correct color or tonal rendition—emulsion speed and emulsion stability are the critical factors in any film, monochrome or color, negative or positive, for wildlife. Emulsion speed very simply makes it possible to take some pictures a slower film would not permit, either due to reduced ambient light levels or the need for high shutter speeds to stop action. The tendency of the long lenses to be relatively slow further compounds the problem.

The matter of emulsion stability is of greater importance in wildlife photography than might occur to most users of film. The nature of this game very frequently takes a photographer into places and climates in which the film cannot be cared for as carefully as we might wish, either before or after exposure. This is a particular problem in Africa, the tropics, and even the southwestern United States, where the weather is hot and refrigeration facilities possibly scarce.

It is a greater problem with color emulsions than with black-and-white, but it has an effect even on the monochrome films. Among the Eastman color positive materials, the Kodachromes are much more heat resistant than the Ektachromes, and some of the latter are more sensitive to high temperatures than others.

Home processing capability is much more important to some photographers than to others. For those who insist on doing their own color developing, the Ektachromes are the only choice among Eastman reversal films, like it or not. All black-and-white emulsions in common use are, of course, easily developed in the home darkroom. The color negative films—Kodacolor and Vericolor—can also be home processed using the C-41 chemistry. The color negative films are, with commercial processing, a pretty expensive way to go unless you order proof-sheets with the processing and have only the best negatives printed. Home processing, therefore, is an attractive idea, but it requires considerably more equipment and

John Wootters often works in black-and-white film, and this shot shows why. The bobcat responded to a predator call on a day so dark that the negatives were overexposed between two and three full stops, even with ASA 400 Tri-X Pan. With any color film, no picture could have been saved, but manipulation in processing the negatives and making the enlargement produced this striking print. (Photo by John Wootters)

technique than black-and-white films, and enlarging gear is more costly.

More specific information and opinions about these various emulsion types will be contributed by each individual author in their separate discussions below. Once more, we'll let Jerry Smith have the first shot.

When I am asked "What kind of film should I use?," I have to ask the inquirer a few questions before I can answer. The answer depends upon his experience, his desires, his equipment, and his intended wildlife subjects. If he is a newcomer, especially to the use of telephoto lenses, and his objective is nice colored prints to show to his friends or to frame, the best answer probably is Eastman Kodacolor II or an equivalent. It has adequate speed (ASA 100) to allow him enough shutter speed to keep camera movement out of his negatives if he's careful, and has very wide exposure latitude, almost two full stops in each direction. I wouldn't be surprised if co-author Wootters disagreed with that word "adequate," however. (Co-author's note: Right!) Besides being a very forgiving film of errors and miscalculations in exposure settings, the color negative Kodacolor II offers nice color rendition, although it is limited in its enlarging abilities and tends to become grainy if blown up a bit too much.

The preferred film for advanced amateurs and professionals, and my own favorite, is Eastman Kodachrome 64, a color positive or transparency film. When K64 was introduced and replaced the old Kodachrome X (ASA 64), my photographs began to improve immensely. This was one of the greatest things which has happened to wildlife photography since I've been in the field. Until then, a photographer using a long telephoto lens had to rely on the beautiful but very slow Kodachrome II (ASA 25) or use the faster but not nearly as high-quality Kodachrome X or Ektachrome X. Using Kodachrome II with a long lens meant shooting at speeds of 1/30th or 1/60th second most of the time and hoping for enough light occasionally to get up to 1/125th. When a photographer successfully recorded a running or flying creature with such a combination, he'd really done something!

Well, we can all give thanks to the Mighty Yellow Father Kodak for the research and development which has given us the most widely-used color slide film, by professionals and amateurs alike. K64 is almost as grainless as its brother K25, and the additional f-stop-plus in emulsion speed is reason enough for sticking with it to the exclusion of all others . . . which is exactly what I do. It's my basic, staple wildlife film, and I very seldom even carry any other kind of film along on field trips.

In reading these comments, one must bear in mind that my wildlife photography goals are, as pointed out in the Preface, somewhat different from those of other photographers. Only the very, very best pictures—technically error-free—are of any professional value to me. My average of

This represents one of those rare
opportunities wherein a motor drive
does pay off. As this pair of pintail
ducks flashed across the frame,
the photographer was too busy
following the focus to try to "time"
the shot. (Photo by Jerry Smith)

"keepers" is probably only one slide per 36-exposure roll, and maybe only one of every 100 exposures will ever be used in any way.

By being this critical of my own work I almost force myself to use Kodachrome 64, which means that I do miss many opportunities in low light situations. It isn't that I don't try to capture that elusive early morning scene; I do! It's just that I don't seem to have a very good success ratio trying to hold a long lens at shutter speeds slower than 1/30th second. But when I do connect, the result makes all the efforts worthwhile!

The nonprofessional who doesn't have to depend on his results for a living can be very well satisfied with one of the faster Ektachrome films to capture the charm of very early morning wildlife activity. This is the period when most creatures are most active and the photographer is most likely to encounter them. If you, like most of us, run into problems with insufficient light for K64 for early morning or late evening shots, you may wish to experiment with something like Ektachrome 200 during these periods and switch to the slower emulsion for midmorning-to-midafternoon.

If you take this approach, don't forget to change the ASA setting of the camera when you switch films. On more than one occasion, I've forgotten this important matter myself and ruined a hard day's work.

Which is one more good reason, for me, to carry and load with just one kind of film and that one will be Kodachrome 64 until something better comes along.

Having said that, Smith now turns it over to Wootters, for a slightly different point of view:

There was a time when amateur photographers shot mostly black-and-white film and professionals tended to use color. Nowadays, that situation has almost completely reversed, and most of the black-and-white being exposed these days is by professional photographers shooting for reproduction in newspapers and magazines. This is exactly my own situation.

As mentioned in the early pages, the majority of my wildlife photographs are used as illustrations of my own articles in various magazines, and are reproduced in black-and-white. Many are converted from color slides, but these are never as good as they could have been if they had originated from high-quality black-and-white negatives. With that in mind, probably 75 percent of my wildlife pictures are made with monochrome film.

This has its advantages, one of which is the relatively high emulsion speeds available in such films. Another is the tremendous latitude of black-and-white films. For comparison, a half-stop over or underexposure with any color film may be enough to ruin the shot; with most black-and-white emulsions, one must err on either side by at least *one full stop* to even notice much difference in density, and I have had pictures published which

Super telephoto lenses like the Questar 700mm are occasionally useful on small subject such as birds when a uniform background is present and enough light exists for their relatively small true apertures. (Photo by Jerry Smith)

This flamboyant green jay, found only along the lower border with Mexico, exhibits all the characteristics of jaybirds everywhere. (Photo by Jerry Smith)

A major asset for any wildlife photographer is an eye for the appealing composition in the commonplace scene or species, like this bright, little cock bobwhite amidst the spring blossoms. (Photo by Jerry Smith)

were originally underexposed by two full stops. This flexibility arises not only from the increased latitude of the film, but the ease with which contrast can be adjusted, first during the development of the film and second during the enlarging process.

One occasion comes to mind when I called up a big bobcat on a very dark, cloudy winter day. To make matters worse, I was located in a shady grove of trees, and using an old Canon 300 mm f / 5.6 lens. The cat put on a real show, boldly walking up to my camouflaged form until he was too close for a focus. The camera's meter sternly warned me that photography was futile in that light, but I shot up a whole roll anyway, and segregated and marked the cassette. The light level was between two and three stops below the indicated optimum, and with Kodachrome film I could only have sat and admired the bobcat.

As it was, I processed that roll of film separately, forcing development to pick up the contrast. The negatives came out a little thin but not bad, and a #4 Polycontrast filter on Eastman Polycontrast Rapid paper did the rest. One of the pictures from that roll appears in this book, and you can judge for yourself the results. The Tri-X film with which I had loaded that day made me money, but even the fastest of the color emulsions would have turned the experience into an interesting adventure in nature watching . . . and a dead loss, financially.

Since 8x10 inches is the largest print for which I have any use, I use Tri-X exclusively, rating it at ASA 320 and developing in Microdol-X diluted 3:1. This gives acceptably fine-grain structure for even the most severe cropping I may need during enlargement. If I went in for photomurals, I'd probably use a finer-grain film. For really big enlargements, Panatomic-X is unbeatable, being as nearly grainless as black-and-white film can get. Properly developed Plus-X Pan is nearly as smooth and provides more contrast, not to mention its great advantage in speed (ASA 125 *vs.* ASA 25 for Panatomic-X).

Tri-X can also be very easily "pushed" during development, to an effective ASA of 800 or even 1200, using Accufine or one of the other "hot" developers. Once in a blue moon, this capability will allow you to record some wildlife behavior you would otherwise not have a prayer of getting. Stretched end-to-end, the 35 mm Tri-X film I've shot would probably reach across Texas . . . and before I'm through, it might reach coast-to-coast!

Like my co-author and most other wildlife photography professionals, I'd have to call Kodachrome 64 my "standard" wildlife color slide film, for all the reasons enumerated in the Introduction section of this chapter. However, when there just isn't enough light for the shutter speed and lens I need, I'm not to proud to switch a faster film, specifically Ektachrome 200.

This dynamic shot of white-fronted geese taking flight was taken with a Canon 500mm "mirror" lens, and shows the virtue of a plain, or uniform, background when using such a lens. (Photo by John Wootters)

It may be that both remarks so far in this chapter have made Ektachrome sound worse than it is, and that's unintentional. Eastman markets *no* unsatisfactory films, when used as and when intended. These are intended to give photographers fast slide films which can be home or custom developed, and they do exactly that. Specifically for wildlife purposes, they are somewhat grainier than the Kodachromes, are much less heat-resistant, and do not have quite the resolution, or sharpness. On the other hand, I have sold a lot of Ektachrome transparencies to discriminating editors, a few of them for use on magazine covers.

The color balance of the Ektachromes, of course, is partly a subjective matter. I, for one, do not find it as pleasing or realistic looking as the rendition of Kodachrome, with a pronounced tendency toward the bluish tints. My experience has been that it has more exposure latitude than Kodachrome, but less color latitude, meaning that exposures must approach perfection fairly closely to achieve a well-balanced rendition.

If you really wish to find out how sharp and grainless a color slide film is, trying to make black-and-white internegatives from it is as good a way as any, and I rarely find that I can do this satisfactorily from Ektachrome transparencies.

Everything said here about Ektachrome 200 applies to Ektachrome 400, only more so. Since the ASA 200 emulsion can be force-developed about one stop, I stick with it and count on pushing it via custom processing if absolutely necessary. All this means that there are always a few rolls of Ektachrome 200 tucked away in my film case (or, more likely, my freezer), and that they produce pictures I could not obtain with the Kodachrome.

An area in which neither my co-author nor I are very experienced is that of the color negative films. My editors want black-and-white prints and color slides, so I have no professional use for the negative films, and neither does Jerry, for similar reasons. They have a certain appeal for me, however, since good monochromatic enlargements are possible on Kodak Panalure paper from the color negatives. Furthermore, Vericolor II Professional Type S is touted as a negative film from which color slides of excellent quality can be produced. All that being true, this film offers the potential of producing good transparencies or either black-and-white or color prints, quite a tall order for one film to fill for a professional in my business. With an ASA rating of 100 (daylight), it has a fine-grain structure and fairly good resolving power (about 80 percent that of Kodachrome 64).

There are two non-professional color negative films in the Kodak stable, Kodacolor II (ASA 100) and Kodacolor 400 (ASA 400). Of the two, I have used the former for documentary-type shots (not wildlife) with pleasing results, but abandoned experiments with the 400 version after a few rolls.

Reflections in water are often a key to an artistic wildlife picture. In this case, the reflection delineates the subject—a whitetail deer— better than the direct image, and projects a nice mood of peace. (Photo by Jerry Smith)

This portrait of an African gray
heron was exposed on
Kodachrome 64 on Lake Kariba, in
what is now called Zimbabwe,
southern Africa.
(Photo by John Wootters)

Given a little cover, many species of prey animals are expert at freezing, remaining undetected by being absolutely motionless . . . at least until the threat comes too near. This black-tailed jackrabbit is doing just that. (Photo by Jerry Smith)

These are the 35mm Kodak films most commonly used by amateur and professional wildlife photographers alike. At left and center, Ektachrome 200 and 400, Kodachrome 64, for slides, and Kodacolor II for color negatives. At right, Plus-X Pan and the faster Tri-X Pan take care of most black-and-white needs. (Photo by John Wootters)

Young wildlife not only doesn't
get an even break; the odds are
stacked against it until it
gains experience, size, and mastery
of its weapons. This coyote
pup, however, already reflects the
wild cunning of its kind.
(Photo by Jerry Smith)

*Quick thinking (to select the
backlighted angle) and exposure
control to produce the silhouette
gets pictures like this one.
(Photo by Jerry Smith)*

Thus far, I have discussed the films of Eastman Kodak exclusively, and must confess that I use them almost exclusively because they're readily available, almost worldwide, and I'm familiar with the compatible chemistry and techniques. I have also shot some Agfa, Ilford, Ansco, and Fuji films, sometimes with very nice results but, so far, none so nice as to cause me to abandon Eastman. But, believe me, if somebody else—*anybody* else—could give me a film with Kodachrome's image characteristics and an ASA rating of at least 160 to 200, I'd switch in a flash!

To show you how far I'm willing to go in that direction, I have experimented with increasing the speed of Kodachrome 64 by a process called "flashing," wherein a portion of the light necessary to correctly expose the film is built into the emulsion by pre-exposing it on an out-of-focus, neutral gray card. Thus the emulsion is preloaded with light but with no latent image. When the film is then exposed on a subject, rated at ASA 200 or even ASA 400, the image is produced with less than the normal amount of light necessary.

Believe it or not, this trick works, and I actually have shot some "Kodachrome 200," achieving good images with normal development. Alas, there are drawbacks, chief among them that an enormous amount of time and work is required. Furthermore, the shelf-life of the "flashed" film is reduced, as one would expect, and so is the apparent exposure latitude—which is already small enough. Finally, there is the problem of registering the film in the camera when it is loaded for the final exposure so that the pre-flashed frames exactly coincide with those which are about to be exposed. This entails counting sprocket holes with great care when loading, and I don't have time for that in the presence of an elusive wild animal!

I should have known it couldn't be that simple; if it were, Kodak would presumably have already done it. Ah, well, we can't have *everything* . . . and we should be grateful that the films which are on the dealer's shelves are as good as they are.

For the very best in technical information about all Kodak films, every photographer should have on hand a current copy of "Kodak Professional Black-and-White Films," Eastman Kodak Publication F-5, and one of "Kodak Color Films for Professional Use," Publication E-77, available at your local camera shop or direct from Eastman Kodak. Don't let the "professional" tags scare you off. Get these and read them, and you'll know *more* than most professionals about Kodak films.

4

Understanding Animal Behavior

Perhaps the single greatest obstacle to successful wildlife photography is that most Americans, sadly enough, obtain their concepts about the nature, habits, and behavior of wild creatures from television and/or an occasional visit to the zoo. Zoo specimens live in a totally artificial environment (however "nice" or "pretty" it may appear to human visitors) and the reactions are abnormal. With a few exceptions, TV programs centering around wild animals are about as true-to-life as Bugs Bunny, Coyote, and Roadrunner.

Even those documentaries which manage a fairly accurate protrayal of the lifestyles of wild animals rarely succeed in conveying to the viewer *why* they do what they do, how they perceive the world in which they live, or anything about the internal population dynamics of the species. Even where the producer is not attempting to peddle a point of view, he simply has not enough time on the air to both entertain and instruct the viewer. At worst, the impressions left by some programs (*Grizzly Adams* was the classic example) are potentially quite dangerous to a wildlife watcher who attempts to deal with animals in a similar manner.

It is best, then, to begin with the advice to forget everything you ever saw on TV pertaining to the habits and reactions of wild animals.

The second step is to make a study of the species available to you for photography from authoritative sources. With hundreds of species of mammals in North America alone, not to mention the birds, reptiles, and amphibians, no one book can even begin to give you insights you need into the natures of all of them. Furthermore, many species have never been comprehensively studied by professionals, and it's quite possible that you may

An alert Mexican ground squirrel stands up to scan the horizon for any of his multitude of enemies. All species have excellent early warning systems and the photographer must learn to circumvent them in order to secure pictures like this.
(Photo by Jerry Smith)

Animal behavior cannot be learned in zoos. This African sitatunga bull, photographed in the San Diego zoo, would be found in marshes and swamps in the wild. He is the most aquatic of the world's true antelopes, and is completely out of character in this picture. (Photo by John Wootters)

witness and even photograph wildlife behavior never before reported by scientists.

The most authoritative source of all is invariably the animal himself. Go and watch him in his natural habitat. Observe his every action and try to understand what he's up to and why. Animals' actions are almost never random; every movement has a purpose and is part of a logical sequence of movements (although the logic is sometimes obscure to a human observer). Understanding these sequences can, obviously, help the photographer to place himself advantageously. If he understands that a whitetail buck's pawing at the earth during the breeding season is a ritualized segment of the animal's effort to attract females in estrous, he will understand that the buck will most likely return to that spot several times a day, handy information for one who wishes to photograph a whitetail buck. If the pawing is as meaningless to the wildlife photographer as it is to most humans (hunters excepted), he may miss a fine opportunity.

One can no more acquire a genuine understanding of the ways and motivations of a wild animal from books and magazines, of course, than he can from TV, but at least the published material will alert one to what to watch for and may help interpret what is seen. Almost any large public library offers a wealth of research material, and we recommend you utilize it as fully as possible. It will shorten the road to good pictures, and lessen the disappointments along the way. Besides, understanding the ways of animals is fun!

Certain information is basic, regardless of the species. Where does it live? What does it eat? Does it migrate, and, if so, when? Is it solitary or is it found in flocks or herds? What sort of sign does it leave? How does it go about the mating process (most species have specific and fascinating rituals, and this is one of the best opportunities for photographs)? How does it relate to others of its own species, and to other species (as predators or prey, for example)? How does it react to different weather conditions? Is it primarily nocturnal or diurnal? Which of its senses is most acute and most relied upon? Is it potentially dangerous to a human? How does it communicate (much animal communication is very subtle, including nuances of body language, use of the eyes, and even changes in color in some portions of the animal's body)?

When you have a reasonably good answer to all these questions about the species of interest to you at the moment, you will be considerably ahead of most newcomers to the wildlife photography field. Striking wildlife pictures very seldom eventuate from wandering around in the woods with a camera in hand; they are, in a way, planned for, at least to the extent that the cameraman intends to see a certain species that day, and has more than a vague hope that the creature will show up in the area he has chosen. The point can hardly be overstressed: every top professional wildlife photographer we know—and that includes most of them currently working— has an expert's knowledge of the animals they photograph most frequently and successfully.

It's important to understand, too, that all living creatures have what biologists call a "fight-or-flight radius." It is the *lebensraum,* or elbow room, each individual creature demands for itself. If a human intrudes within that radius, the animal will either flee or, if this is its temperament, charge the intruder. The sad fact is that the longest telephoto lens is not usually sufficient to get good pictures of the critter from outside this radius. We have to figure out ways to get *inside* it, and much of this book is devoted to such means.

The fight-or-flight radius varies very widely, even with any given individual animal, and the variations depend on a multitude of unpredictable factors. A

All creatures have what is called a "fight-or-flight" radius, into which a photographer cannot intrude without provoking either one reaction or the other. The erected bristles of this javelina, plus an emission of skunk-like musk from a gland above the tail, clearly signals that he's ready to flee. Especially with potentially dangerous species, the photographer must be alert to these signals. (Photo by John Wootters)

Mating rituals of many species are dramatic and seldom photographed. Here, Jerry Smith belly-crawls close enough to photograph two entirely different rituals in the same frame—a pair of axis deer bucks fighting savagely for dominance and an oblivious wild turkey gobbler in full strut to impress a nearby hen.
(Photo by Mike Alebis)

mother bear with cubs, for example, will not permit a male bear anywhere near her, yet, during the breeding season, she may solicit his company. Whitetail bucks form very close-knit bachelor clubs during the summer months, but may fight their summertime buddies savagely over breeding territory during the rut. A thirsty animal in a drought will approach a human waiting at a waterhole with a camera much more closely than it would under other circumstances. Most wildlife can be ''tamed'' by artificial feeding to permit a much closer approach by humans than the same animal will allow by the same human *away from the feeding place.*

In other words, the invisible boundaries of each creature's personal space expand and contract according to location, the identity of the intruder, the presence of young, the habituation of the animal to food, water, and human presence, season, hormonal factors, and many others. The photographer may know enough about the species, or a familiar individual of the species, to have a general idea of what to expect, but no man can predict exactly how any animal will react on any given occasion.

With practice, however, he can learn to read an animal's reactions and know about where he'd better stop in his approach. As he approaches the boundary of the fight-or-flight zone, the animal will exhibit increasing signs of nervousness . . . but every species has a different way of signaling nervousness. For example, if you begin to walk straight toward a whitetail buck in an area where the deer is not accustomed to being threatened by humans, he will stand and stare at you, head up and ears cocked in your direction. As you come closer and closer, his tail will begin to switch more and more frequently, and the long white hairs on his rump under the tail will begin to erect and flare outward. His body will grow more and more tense, and he will probably lift a forefoot, hold it poised, and then stamp the ground. Eventually, one or both ears will roll to the rear, and you can expect him to burst into flight within seconds of that action.

There are ways, however, to hold him there a little longer. One is to approach obliquely, never walking straight toward your subject, but angling to one side or another, pretending to pay no attention whatever to him. Another is to stop whenever his nervousness appears to be getting close to the breaking point and direct your attention somewhere else for a few minutes, watching the buck only out of the corner of your eye. When his suspicions seem to be partly allayed, take a few more steps. A direct, frontal approach, a stealthy approach (hiding behind bushes as you come), and a direct gaze are all associated in any prey animal's mind with predators.

Some people seem to have an instinctive knack for approaching animals without alarming them, and we have often wondered about this. I (Woot-

Birds of prey are the champion ''seers'' of the animal kingdom. This young redtail hawk actually does possess magnifying eyeballs which enlarge images about 50 percent. (Photo by Jerry Smith)

With experience, it's possible to "shadow" an animal until he becomes somewhat habituated to the photographer's presence. It's a favorite technique of many expert wildlife lensmen, including Jerry Smith, shown here tailing a chital, or Indian axis deer buck. (Photo by Mike Alebis)

ters) believe that all mammals and some birds, at least, are able to read a human's unconscious body langauge with surprising accuracy. Just as a dog or horse will surely know whether you are afraid of him merely by watching you from a distance, my theory is that a deer or crow also can sense whether you mean him harm through subtle signals of which you are not aware, and which cannot be faked. This is why photographers often find it easy to get much closer to animals than hunters do, and how it is possible for a photographer who is patient simply to follow an animal or a herd around at a respectful distance, making no effort at concealment, until the creatures cease to pay much attention to him. Many of the great wildlife pictures of recent times were secured in just this way, and it is a favorite technique of Jerry Smith with the big whitetail bucks for which he is famous.

John Wootters once won a bet that he could walk, in plain sight, from one end of a 15-acre oat field in which several whitetail does were feeding to the other without causing any of them to leave the field. This was in an area which was regularly hunted and the deer were as wild as any deer can be. He succeeded by the patient use of all the techniques mentioned above, never looking at the deer directly, never walking straight toward them, stopping whenever their signs of nervousness seemed to approach the critical point, and just being casual in his movements.

Most beginners at this business are astonished at what can be done around wild animals by a photographer who understands their habits and reactions.

So far, we've been talking about the "flight" part of the reaction, but a word on the "fight" part is in order. Wildlife photography is not a dangerous sport, provided the photographer has a rudimentary grasp of how animals react, but cameramen can and have been seriously injured and even killed when they didn't. There are a few rules. First, never trust any large wild animal completely, to the extent of placing yourself at his mercy should he become frightened or angry. Second, never trust any male animal during the rutting season. Third, never trust any female with young. Finally, never make any animal feel cornered.

Careful observance of these rules will avoid most problems, but it is well to bear in mind that an animal doesn't think like a man, and what *you* think of as provocation and what *he* thinks of as provocation may be two entirely different things. To an African elephant your mere existence, within 100 yards or so, may draw a serious charge, and the same is true of the African lion. Elephant cows with small calves may actually charge a whiff of your scent, without seeing you at all.

I have seen a foolish photographer in Yellowstone Park charged by a bull bison, and I have myself been charged by a buffalo cow with a newborn calf

Familiarity with the creature's senses and how he uses them will help the cameraman get within range. Here, author Smith takes advantage of a peccary's poor eyesight to approach quietly upwind. The nearsighted beast has just noticed a new element in his environment and his erected bristles indicate his sudden suspicion and alarm. *(Photo by Mike Alebis)*

Although anthropomorphizing never does wildlife a service, sometimes animals' expressions and body language seem so human that it's difficult to resist, as in the case of this amorous whitetail buck receiving a distinct brush-off from his intended mate.
(Photo by John Wootters)

(which I hadn't even seen). Female elk and especially moose with small calves can be quite nasty, and sow bears with cubs can be downright fatal to a photographer who means their babies no harm whatever. I have also seen a female collared peccary offer to fight three grown men to get to her two tiny babies, although she couldn't have weighed 30 pounds. She left no doubt she meant business, and we very respectfully stood to one side.

A number of people have been killed by "pet" whitetail bucks which were maddened by the rutting instinct, and the most recent of these of which we are aware was a wildlife photographer who entered a large pen at that time of year. Bull moose have been known to try to fight a freight train when in that mood, so a guy with a camera wouldn't seem too formidable to 1,200 pounds of enraged moose.

There are other things which can happen. When Wootters was taking game pictures in Mozambique's Gorangoza Park in 1972, a couple of German girls drove their rented Volkswagen between a bull hippopotamus and his waterhole, and were found, uninjured but terrified, in their car, which was upside down, hours later. It is also possible that an animal may be rabid, or may have been injured and nursing a grudge against all humans, like a Cape buffalo bull that Wootters encountered in southern Africa which had been wounded by a native poacher's musket ball. The point is that the photographer cannot know everything about a creature's mood, and it pays not to take very much for granted. Even the larger birds of prey can be very formidable in defense of their nests.

As it's extremely difficult to explain to a large, angry beast that all you wanted was his picture, especially while running as hard as you can, we urge alertness and a healthy dose of prudence in dealing with large game; readers are too hard to find, and we do not wish to lose even one!

A photographer, to get within range of any animal, must deal with the creature's early warning systems, which are his senses. Too many, especially beginners, seem to believe that animals' senses are just about like those of humans, and used in much the same way. As a general rule, it's better to assume that the target animal can hear and smell you a mile away and that he can see you through a thin rock. He can't, but it's a worse mistake to underestimate him than to overestimate his capabilities. Even when you try, you'll find it's not easy to overestimate the acuity of wildlife's sensory perceptions. Anyone with a dog around the house, of course, already knows that his hearing is much more sensitive than theirs, and that his scenting ability is simply incomprehensible to a human. The dog's master, however, probably doesn't know *how much* better the animal's hearing is than his own; the mutt can not only hear sound frequencies both above and below the range of the normal human ear, but he can hear much less

A basic rule for locating wildlife is to look for the target animal's food sources . . . whether a grizzly bear's snowberry bushes or a bumblebee's nectar. (Photo by Mike Alebis)

An understanding of the social
behavior of wild animals is
invaluable to the photographer.
Many species have greeting rituals
based on the relative dominance,
or place in the "pecking order," of
the individuals involved. Of these
whitetail bucks, the one on the right
is dominant, as shown by the angle
at which he presents his antlers to
the other. (Photo by Jerry Smith)

noisy noises and, to top it off, can accurately pinpoint the direction of a sound about four times more precisely than can a human. Most wild mammals' hearing is approximately that good, and in some cases better.

We have long believed that most mammals, other than the Primate family to which we ourselves belong, are color-blind, and for all practical purposes we probably can continue to operate as though it were true. However, recent research has proven the presence of a few cone (color sensitive) cells in the retinas of a deer's eye, so we'll have to rethink the question. It is absolutely true, however, that that same deer's eye contains many more and more densely-packed rod cells, which provide black-and-white vision and, especially, poor light vision. A deer, and most other North American mammals, can see a man under twilight conditions in which the deer is invisible, or nothing more than a shapeless blob, to the man.

Some animals—pronghorn antelope and mountain sheep, for examples—have eyes which resolve images at great distances so finely that it is

This New Mexico badger, poking his head out of his hole in a snowy field, looks cute, but his "fight-or-flight" zone has been penetrated by the photographer and he's considering which course of action to take. (Photo by John Wootters)

as though they were looking at you through binoculars, being able to see details at about eight times the distances you and I can. The eyes of some hawks actually do magnify the images about 50 percent. Many prey animals almost literally have eyes in the backs of their heads; the bulging, side-mounted eyes of a cottontail rabbit can simultaneously see all that goes on around him except for about 15 degrees of the 360-degree circle.

All birds, as far as we know, have excellent color vision, which is why you don't see any duck hunters wearing bright red clothing like deer hunters. And owls and a few other night-flying birds can see, on a moonless, starlit night, about as well as you and I can on a dull, overcast day.

Furthermore, many creatures have senses which are so alien to us that they seem supernatural. The poisonous pit-viper snakes—rattlers, copperheads, and cottonmouth moccasins in North America—have organs which can sense infrared (heat) radiation in a directional manner, like our eyes sense visible light. Some sharks, at least, can sense and home in on tiny electrical discharges in the water. Fish and, we are convinced, many other forms of life, possess some mechanism for sensing changes in barometric pressure; they always know about oncoming weather fronts long before the human forecasters can predict them. Other species have incredibly delicate sensitivity to vibrations transmitted through the earth or water.

It is quite possible, too, that there is a sort of "sixth sense" for danger possessed by many mammals (probably including man, in an atrophied sort of way) which is totally beyond the ability of science even to define, much less explain. We have heard theories such as brain waves or inadvertant telepathic communication between predators and prey.

The reason for these few notes on how animals perceive their surroundings is to convince the neophyte wildlife photographer that he's up against some unbelievable capabilities in his would-be subjects, and that he will do well to give a great deal of consideration to ways and means of circumventing or defeating the animals' senses. They are not supernatural, although they often seem so to us, and such ways and means do exist, as we shall see, but they must be given all due respect in your maneuverings in the woods to bring your lenses to bear. Otherwise, you may never get close enough to a critter to use all that fancy equipment we discussed in earlier chapters, except by accident. And great wildlife shots are almost never accidental!

The unusual action is always turning up by surprise before the wildlife photographer. This whitetail buck has recently stripped the velvet from his new antlers but is having trouble getting rid of a couple of tenacious strips of dried skin. Here he's kicking at them with a hind hoof in annoyance, offering an interesting change from the usual head-high portrait. (Photo by Jerry Smith)

5

How To See Animals

*I*n order to take a photograph of a wild animal, it is first necessary to be aware of its presence. Although it is not uncommon to hear or even to smell a creature before seeing it, most of us will first perceive the majority of the wild animals we encounter via our sense of sight.

To the inexperienced, those two sentences will seem to be an elementary restatement of the obvious, but the fact is that simply seeing an animal, even one which is more or less in plain sight, is neither as automatic nor as easy as may be believed by persons who have spent most of their lives in civilization.

It is, in fact, a familiar and frustrating experience to every professional hunting guide to have a client completely unable to see a fine trophy animal standing within easy range and plain view, despite all efforts to point it out.

Assuming normal eyesight, such an experience arises from literally not knowing how to see. Effective use of our eyes in the woods is *not* an instinctive skill; it must be acquired through practice. People who live or work in the woods—ranchers, loggers, foresters, trappers, etc.—acquire the knack unconsciously (at least, some of them do). City dwellers' eyes, however, are tuned and trained to an entirely different set of needs. They will see things which are customary, necessary, and important to their daily comings and goings but which the keen-eyed woodsman may overlook entirely on a trip to the city. He may spot a well-camouflaged animal in a thicket instantly, but he may miss a stoplight or a "No Left Turn" sign completely in the confusion of downtown traffic to which he is not accustomed.

By the same token, the townsman may stare at that thicket, in which he's

Even large animals can be very difficult to spot by the inexperienced observer, until he learns to look for bits and pieces of animals instead of whole forms. (Photo by Jerry Smith)

*Small deer fawns are extremely hard
to locate and are easily frightened.
But when the chance to photograph
a pair of tiny twins like this comes
along, the result is sure to melt
the heart of every nature lover.
(Photo by Jerry Smith)*

This grizzly bear in the Canadian Rockies gives us an example of the "in-habitat" shot, wherein the animal is really more an element in the composition than its feature. Such pictures show us how the animal fits into, moves around in and appears in his natural environment. (Photo by John Wootters)

been told a deer is standing, for half an hour and never pick it out until it moves. It happens all the time. He simply doesn't know what to look for or where to look for it. His eye isn't trained to identify a line, a half-seen mass, or a shadow amid a confusion of similar forms, or how to interpret correctly the information forwarded to his brain by his optic nerves. Out of our respective elements, all of us have difficulty at first, both in visual acquisition of data and with the interpretation thereof.

The non-woodsman, therefore, who wishes to launch into wildlife photography suffers under a very fundamental handicap; unless a creature is in motion or in an unusually conspicuous situation, he may have trouble spotting the beast within the relatively brief time period available to bring his camera to bear, after said beast has seen him.

Fortunately, most of us are able to develop our powers of observation, with conscious effort. Two major areas are involved, the first being the improved use of our *peripheral* vision, and the second is rapid and comprehensive assimilation of detail in a given scene. Having learned to use our

Spotting whole animals in the open is easy . . . but, alas, not very common with most woodland species. In this picture, one buck is conspicuous, and the second is easily seen because the eye is drawn to him by the first. But can you see the third one? (Photo by Jerry Smith)

One must look for wild subjects where they wish to be, and not where the photographer wishes them to be. That means learning the essentials of each species' habitat, in terms of cover, seasonal food resources, water, and other special requirements (such as roosting trees for wild turkeys). (Photo by Jerry Smith)

eyes in a wildlife setting, it is then necessary to teach ourselves what to look for and, just as important, where to look for it. A quick illustration will suffice: a whitetail or mule deer buck, a big one, stands only about thigh-high to a grown man at his shoulders, with the highest tips of his antlers about breast-high to the same man, when his head is erect (which it seldom is). Thus, to spot such an animal in his habitat, one's eyes must sweep the thickets at a level about three feet high. Many newcomers to the game can't see the deer that's in plain sight in the shadows simply because they're looking right over his back, at a height which would be correct for a horse, or a moose, or a greater kudu!

Getting back to peripheral vision, however, most human beings see clearly in an arc of about 25 degrees on each side of a point on which the eyes are focused. This combined arc of 50 degrees, by the way, approximates the field of a so-called "normal" camera lens. Small horizontal eye movements may be unconsciously performed to cover the full 50 degrees.

For most of us, there is another 65 degrees or so on each side of center within which we can perceive movement, color, mass, and contrasting light values, but where these things are not seen in sharp detail. Thus, our full visual field is more like 180 degrees than the original 45 to 50, and this extra arc totaling about 130 degrees is of enormous value in "target acquisition"—initial perception of the presence of a wild creature. Most of the animals and birds we seek to film, incidentally, have much wider visual fields than we do; some of them have at least some vision around the entire 360-degree circle and a few, like the American woodcock, actually have *binocular* vision straight to the rear as well as to the front. Needless to say, these visual assets and others discussed elsewhere, have survival value in the wild world. We can never match them, but it behooves every camera hunter to develop what he does possess to the maximum, if he is to deal with such critters.

How can one actually learn to see, and how can progress be measured? Try the following: while walking along the street, select a certain display window in a store and pause in front of it for about 30 seconds, noting as many details of the merchandise on display and decorative elements as possible. Then, at the first opportunity, try to write down literally everything you saw in the window. Unless you're already a trained observer, you'll probably be astonished at how much you missed when you compare your list to the actual window display.

Doing this sort of thing daily will bring about a rapid and marked improvement in what you have heretofore taken for granted as your natural ability to see what there is to be seen. You may even come to make a game of it, using pictures in magazines, the clothing and jewelry of your fellow work-

This great blue heron against the setting sun creates a potent mood in color—even though only one color, orange, is actually present. *(Photo by Jerry Smith)*

The universal appeal of baby animals is illustrated by this bobcat kitten. (Photo by Jerry Smith)

The innocence of all wild animals radiates from this tiny whitetail fawn, and suffuses this picture with a feeling of the world as it was before man came into it. (Photo by Jerry Smith)

Backlighting halos the texture of the velvet on this whitetail's antlers in midsummer. (Photo by Jerry Smith)

A grizzly bear, monarch of the mountains, pauses beside a brook. Such beasts are unpredictable and dangerous when in their natural habitat. Extreme care must be exercised by any outdoor photographer. (Photo by John Wootters)

ers, the front page of the newspaper, and many other tests. Make no mistake about it, this is harder work than it sounds, but as your observational capacity improves, you'll find a new pleasure in your heightened awareness of the world around you.

You will, furthermore, see a lot more animal life during your photo excursions into the outdoors. This habit of observation soon becomes just that—an unconscious habit. If the senior author may be permitted a first person tale:

I was walking down an overgrown old roadway in the thickets of east Texas, thinking about anything but deer one day, when I was frozen in midstride by the realization that I had just seen a deer. I couldn't actually remember exactly what I had seen, but my brain had registered deer sometime within my last few steps. I began very slowly to back up, searching the maze of dense foliage, probing with my eyes into every nook and cranny of the thicket. Ten steps backward, and I saw it again—just three black dots visible through a tiny hole in the brush, a pair of eyes and a shiny black nose. I literally couldn't make out another hair on the animal's body, no ears, no neck, no antlers. The black eyes stared into mine for a long second and then simply vanished, and the thicket was so dense that I never caught so much as a glimpse of movement. It was an eerie adventure in observation, almost like *deja vu.*

My eyes had been automatically scanning my environment as I moved quietly along the old roadway, and had registered that triangular pattern of dots as something that didn't belong in that background. My brain then said "deer," or, at least, "suspected deer," although I was literally unconscious of actually having seen the thing that arrested my attention.

That phrase above—". . . something that didn't belong . . ."—is a major key to spotting wildlife. Many newcomers to the woods overlook rather obvious deer because they're looking for a deer. But, unless it's moving, one very rarely sees a whole deer at first; the trick is to look for pieces and parts which don't appear to have grown there. The first perception of a deer is far more frequently nothing more than a horizontal line—the animal's back—in a forest of verticals, the angle of a hind leg, a white patch which turns out to be the lining of an ear, or, as mentioned above, a pair of dark eyes. Sometimes it's merely a block of color, or a shadow . . . something, anything that creates a subtle disturbance in the patterns of trunks, limbs, leaves, grass, and bushes. Maybe nothing more noticeable than a difference in textures, fur against tree bark, for example.

Although it is accepted as an article of faith by hunters, most non-hunters have trouble believing that the way to see an animal in his natural habitat is not to look for the animal, or at least for the whole animal. Believe it; it will

Besides making a pretty composition, this pollen-daubed bee in a cactus blossom tells a story about the interrelationships of different species within an ecosystem.
(Photo by Jerry Smith)

Bees making their rounds among spring flowers are standard subjects for wildlife cameramen, and never fail to delight the eye of the beholder.
(Photo by Jerry Smith)

A male jackrabbit, right, tries to
ingratiate himself with a female,
and every human being who sees
this picture will be able to
identify with one or the other.
(Photo by Jerry Smith)

Proposed by Benjamin Franklin for the national bird of the United States, the wild turkey lost out to the bald eagle . . . but makes a majestic subject for the wildlife photographer. (Photo by Jerry Smith)

get you some picture opportunities your unbelieving friends would never notice!

The next step is learning where to look, within the habitat, for the target creature. With a few exceptions—pronghorn antelope, bison, and caribou among them, in America—most mammals spend very little time during daylight in the open. They inhabit what biologists refer to as "edge habitat," which means the narrow strips where two different kinds of habitat meet. An example is where a woods border an open field or meadow. Whitetail deer, for example, will not be seen standing out in the open meadow very often, nor will they often be found deep in the heart of a large forest. Look for them within a hundred yards on either side of that "edge," most often inside the first screens of brush, during daylight.

On Wootters' first safari in Africa, in Mozambique in 1972, the white hunter expressed surprise at the ability of Wootters and his companion to spot African game, especially since they often couldn't even identify the species of animal they'd spotted. Wootters explained, "Well, we're both old whitetail hunters in the U.S. and have the habit of looking for bits and pieces of animals, back in the edges of the thickets, instead of whole animals standing in the open."

It was a great truth, and one that every wildlife photographer will benefit greatly from learning.

On that same safari, the senior author was astonished at how difficult it can be to see an elephant in heavy woods. The problem was the reverse of looking over a deer's back; he was scanning at the level his American training had taught him, and all he was seeing was elephant legs, which look remarkably like tree trunks when motionless. When he realized that a big African bull elephant may stand 11 or 12 feet high at the shoulders and made the necessary adjustment, he began seeing the great beasts, but, even then, found them considerably less conspicuous in their habitat than seems possible.

It may seem obvious that one looks for squirrels in trees, for turtles in the water, and for deer on the ground, but there is more to it than that. One looks for squirrels in certain kinds of trees, and not in others, for the most part. Hardwood trees, especially in ancient stands where the trees probably have hollows for denning, and mast-bearing groves will produce gray and fox squirrels 10 to 1 over pines, for example, especially where pines have little or no understory of shrubs beneath them. Where pines and hardwoods occur in mixed stands, the hardwoods tend to be found in the "bottoms," while the pines command the uplands.

Most aquatic species—turtles, water snakes, frogs, and so forth—need more or less permanent water to make a home, and temporary catchments rarely exist long enough for the necessary ecological chains to be forged for a true habitat. The more mobile a species, the more likely he is to be found in some temporary situation (within their range and habitats, birds may be spotted almost anywhere, for example, while reptiles are quite closely bound to their specific territories), but the photographer who devotes his time to the likeliest areas will be far ahead of the game, both figuratively and literally.

We will have a good deal more to say along these lines in the next chapter, and about concealing oneself from prospective subjects in subsequent ones, but, before we close this chapter, a few notes may be in order about one's own mode of movement.

Striding boldly around in wild animal habitat is not a very good way to see a lot of game. Taking pains to move slowly and quietly, with frequent pauses, is infinitely more productive. The reason is that in this contest of eyes, the creature that's moving is at a disadvantage to the one that's motionless. Not only do all mammalian eyes pick up movement more quickly and positively than they do mere stationary shapes (including ours), but they do not register even a moving form as readily when they are

To the inexperienced woodland observer, it's beyond belief that he could walk past an animal in plain sight and fail to see it . . . but the authors have seen it happen time and again. Looking comes naturally, but seeing takes practice. (Photo by John Wootters)

103

One of the fiercest animals in North America is the great horned owl, the tiger of the skies. This bird will defend its nest savagely, and should be treated with profound respect by the photographer. (Photo by Jerry Smith)

Here author Wootters has approached a deer by advancing when the buck's head was down, grazing, and "freezing" when the animal lifted his head to look around. As long as movement is directly toward the animal and he doesn't catch you in motion, this can be quite successful. (Photo by Jerry Smith)

This is the first picture taken during the above episode. The buck has just decided that there's something fishy about that peculiar "stump" and has stopped chewing to study it suspiciously. (Photo by John Wootters)

themselves in motion. Therefore, walking slowly and stopping often to survey the surroundings while remaining motionless will produce at least double the sightings you'll have while just strolling along.

Furthermore, many of the animals you do see while walking will not be seen until it's far too late to secure a photograph, after the creature has panicked and is in full flight into or through heavy cover.

All wild animals have developed the strategy of "freezing" in order to avoid detection to a high art, and it is especially effective against the human animal, who tends to be nervous and impatient by nature. Wild creatures have no sense of the passage of time, time itself being a strictly human invention, while we are cursed with a lively ability to become bored in a hurry. It is an advantage our wild subjects have over us as photographers.

It can also work in our favor, in one way, though, and that chance comes when an animal which has "frozen" at our approach can be spotted before he moves and convinced that we have not noticed him. As long as we do not alter our rythmn of movement and do not look pointedly at him, we may be able to pass quite close to him, but within seconds of the moment we stop and turn toward him, he will explode into flight. Those seconds, however, can be very productive with a little attention to prefocusing and exposure setting before we raise the lens in his direction.

Another useful trick takes advantage of the difficulty most mammals have in making sense of a motionless object. The authors have often gotten quite close to an animal with a direct approach, by moving only when the subject's head was down, grazing, or its attention directed elsewhere. The technique requires that we move straight toward the creature, and freeze instantly when it looks in our direction, remaining absolutely motionless while it studies us. Eventually, it will go back to feeding or whatever and look away, at which time we make another cautious advance. This is delicate work, but it's a lot of fun and will sometimes get a shot that's otherwise hopeless. The accompanying pictures show Wootters playing this game with a whitetail buck caught feeding in the open in high grass, and the resulting pictures. The deer's vision was blocked by the grass as he fed on low-growing forbs, allowing Wootters to gain a few steps between the times he raised his head to look around for danger. On each look around he would stare suspiciously at this peculiar, motionless object, but he could not perceive that it was a little closer each time he looked. When the motor drive started clicking and whirring, at a distance of a few yards, the buck almost turned inside out. The sequence was photographed from a distance by Jerry Smith.

The photographer who learns patience and the arts of inconspicuousness from his wild subjects will find a multitude of ways to succeed.

When the author's motor drive started whirring, the buck's worst suspicions were confirmed, with this result. (Photo by John Wootters)

6

Where To Find Subjects

Finding something at which to point a lens would appear to be pretty basic to the wildlife photography process, and we are occasionally astonished at the number of photographers who seem not to realize that it's a problem. It is, in fact, *the* single greatest problem in wildlife photography! When you have located a potential subject—that is, when you have him in sight—about 90 percent of the battle is won. Compared to finding him, taking his picture is usually relatively simple.

If you look at the distribution or range maps for a given species of wildlife in a field guide or identification manual, you may discover that the animal's range seems to cover several entire states. If you go into the field in any of those states, however, you're sure to find that there are a lot more places where your beast is *not* than where he *is*. Certain species, of course, are more ubiquitous than others, because the ecological niche they occupy is much broader than is the case with other species. That simply means their habitat needs are less specialized, and, usually, that their reproductive rate is high enough to furnish populations to occupy every available habitat. The cottontail rabbit is an example.

Of the larger animals, the whitetail deer, raccoon, and coyote are remarkably adaptable. Any of these species can and do live in swamps, deserts, high mountain ranges, coastal islands, heavily-populated farmlands, and even inside major cities. The senior author resides miles inside the city limits of the largest city in the South, and as these words are being written there are 18 raccoons eating dog food in his backyard.

On the other hand, if photographs of otters, muskrats, or nutria, for example, are on your agenda, you'll be wasting your time looking for a

Inca doves at leisure. Note the small, doughnut-shaped highlights characteristic of all ''mirror-type'' telephoto lenses. This was taken through a Canon 500mm SSC. (Photo by John Wootters)

Most—but not all—animals and birds need to drink, and regular waterholes are excellent places to watch during the periods of the day when the target species usually waters, especially in areas where secluded, dependable water sources are scarce. Here author Smith waylays a wild turkey at a pond in late evening. (Photo by Mike Alebis)

subject very far from permanent water. In other words, within those broad shaded regions on the distribution maps, most species will be found only within their own, specialized habitats.

A "habitat" is simply an area which furnishes the animal with all his basic needs. These are food; water (in some form, but not always open surface water); cover (shelter from the elements and from his enemies); the companionship of his own kind, at least now and then; and a suitable place to rear the young. Some species have additional, specialized needs, such as trees of a certain kind, size, and age, gravel for birds' gizzards, and so forth. Sometimes two species which are quite similar in most characteristics will have completely opposite requirements.

Take the pronghorn antelope and whitetail deer. They are both ungulate quadrupeds of about the same size and shape, and can eat many of the same foods. The pronghorn, however, relies almost entirely upon his fantastic eyesight and equally fantastic speed afoot to escape predators, so he lives mostly on open plains where he can see forever and run in any direction. Since he can run faster than any other four-footed North American mammal, all he asks is a running start, and his eyes give him that. He doesn't care whether a predator can see him, as long as he can see the predator, and, as a result, the pronghorn is very conspicuous in his prairie habitat, easy to see but damned hard to approach! The physiologically similar whitetail, on the other hand, is a hider and skulker, never found on open, treeless prairies. He has the nerve to stand stock-still and allow a human to walk past him within a few yards if he has a little cover, and then crouch and almost crawl silently away. Although he's a pretty fair runner in his own right, he rarely runs more than 100 yards, because he's rarely more than that distance from cover. A whitetail, by the way, may live his whole life within a few hundred yards of the spot where he was born, and cannot be permanently driven out of that home territory unless the habitat itself is destroyed.

A big whitetail buck can clear a seven-foot fence in a standing high jump without a second thought, but a pronghorn buck will not even jump over an ordinary livestock fence. It all comes back to the point that we must know something about the species we seek, in order to make an intelligent effort to find him.

Some habitat preferences among wildlife are utterly mysterious to a human. Obviously, one looks for waterfowl and wading birds around water, but certain other birds will be found *only* in thickets, others *only* on grassy prairies, and others *only* in mature evergreen forests. Wootters' backyard is undisturbed riverine woods, while his front yard is more typical suburbia, conventionally landscaped and quite open. Although there obviously is some overlap, a list of bird species sighted in the backyard is quite different from a similar list in the frontyard. The difference is habitat, although both kinds of habitat are confined to a single city lot of about half an acre.

There may also be seasonal differences in where animals are found. The most radical example is migration. During the summer, you may spot a certain species of bird very commonly in a given area, but six months later the nearest live specimen of that bird may be literally thousands of miles away. Or, if you happen to live in neither the breeding nor wintering range of a bird but somewhere in between, you may see him only for a period of two weeks to a month while the migration is passing through in each direction.

Many mammals migrate, as well. Mountain game tends to summer at or above timberline and migrate to wintering grounds in the valleys when the snow gets deep, so the migration may be both vertical and horizontal. The migrations of caribou, whales, lemmings, and various African plains species, such as wildebeests, are famous. Predators usually follow their prey's migrations, too.

Most of what we call "migrations" are movements to fresh food sources, usually over what seem to us to be significant distances. However, all animals move about within their home territories to exploit seasonal food sources, tending to concentrate temporarily in those areas offering abundant forage. The photographer who found a certain species easy to locate

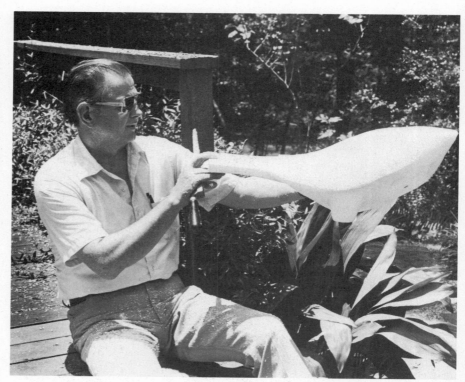

Here author Wootters shapes a block of styrofoam into a wild turkey decoy, using a Surform rasp. The long neck and head will be carved from balsa wood for extra strength and dowelled in place, and half-inch dowels will serve as detachable legs. Before painting, the styrofoam will be protected with a coat of orange shellac. Almost any kind of bird or animal decoy can be improvised quite effectively from styrofoam, including any which cannot be purchased commercially. (Photo by Jeanne Wootters)

Some wildlife pictures are pleasant
to look at merely because of
the mood they project. This heron
winging his way across a marsh
at sunset conveys a powerful
sense of tranquillity.
(Photo by Jerry Smith)

Great blue herons are not commonly found on ocean beaches, except where shallow salt water estuaries are separated from the sea by narrow barrier islands. This one was photographed against the rolling surf along Texas' Padre Island, in just such a situation. (Photo by Jerry Smith)

during the summer may be puzzled at the total absence of that same herd in the same places during the winter. No herbivorous animal utilizes exactly the same resources year 'round, and most of them are capable of using a surprisingly wide variety of plant types. It's necessary to know his diet in some detail to predict where within his home range an animal may be spending most of his time in a certain month.

An example is the season when mast (wild fruits and nuts) is abundant. At this season, in a good year, an entire population may be densely concentrated in a small area abounding with the acorns, grapes, berries, or whatever, but when the bounty is gone, so will the animals be elsewhere. The same may be true where wildlife subsists heavily on agricultural crops at certain times of year.

Likewise, time of year may influence *when* the animals are to be found in their favorite areas. During the wintertime, the collared peccary, or "javelina," ranges about all day long, but during the crushing heat of summer in his subtropical habitat, the little pigs become mostly nocturnal, and will seem to be scarce even in areas where they are known to be plentiful. Many other mammalian species react similarly to hot weather.

Some Canadian and Alaskan species of big game are tormented during summer by flies and mosquitoes (as are wildlife photographers in those latitudes) and seek exposed points and peaks where the wind keeps the insects away. If the bugs are bugging you as you search the shady, lakeside coverts, you're probably looking in the wrong places.

Many kinds of birds and a few mammals tend to congregate for mating and young-rearing, usually on traditional grounds. If the photographer can locate a prairie chicken "booming ground" during the spring breeding season, he will have a wealth of opportunities for unusual and interesting pictures available at no other time or place. Similarly, water birds which nest in colonies or rookeries offer great photo opportunities. Some gregarious bird species also roost in great flocks, using the same areas night after night. Among these are wild turkeys, crows, ravens, many wading birds and carrion-eaters, and some species of doves and pigeons, as well as blackbirds and grackles.

A word the wildlife photographer should be familiar with is "microhabitat," which refers to very specialized and usually small habitat niches occupied by a certain species. An example is the red-cockaded woodpecker, which nests only in ancient pines afflicted with red-heart disease. Another is the golden-cheeked warbler, which nests only in mature junipers in a few very small areas which are entirely surrounded by vast reaches of apparently identical habitat. Certain salamanders, among other species, are found only in the total darkness of a few limestone caves and nowhere

else. Other species are tied to a certain type of soil, a single species of vegetation or animal food (as the everglades kite), or some other equally narrow aspect of a microhabitat. Find that specific set of conditions, and you'll find that animal.

Many forms of wildlife, however, are associated with one set of conditions in one part of the country, and an entirely different set elsewhere. Whitetail deer in south Texas are found nearly everywhere, but spend more time in mesquite-hackberry drainages on sandy loam soil than anywhere else. The same species in northern Michigan haunts white cedar swamps. The photographer must understand the needs of his target species in his own areas, and can be misled by perfectly authentic reports concerning some other part of the country.

A wildlife photographer will benefit greatly from cultivation of the ancient hunters' arts of reading sign—tracks, droppings, the leavings from feeding activities, evidences of mating rituals, and so forth. Most species—even reptiles and insects—leave signs of their passing, and knowing where a certain creature has recently been may be of assistance in predicting where he can be found in the future, since many animals are very much creatures of habit.

There is no magic to reading sign, although it often appears somewhat arcane to the uninitiated. Everybody has eyes, and can learn where to direct them to spot the signs of wildlife in the woods. Experience and observation does the rest. The important thing is to *try,* rather than to assume that tracking and sign reading is something only African bushmen and Apache Indians are good at.

As we have said before, securing good wildlife images is a great deal more than wandering around in the woods "looking for animals." The successful photographer always knows what sort of creature he's out to shoot on that day, and will usually return with film exposed, mostly, on that species. To that end, he goes where he has good reason to expect the subject to be at that time of year, under those weather conditions, and at that hour.

Certainly it is true that the serendipitous appearance occasionally occurs and the lensman grabs the chance to photograph the unexpected species. This sort of thing happens, particularly, in waterhole blinds, or in areas with a bumper crop of some seasonal food utilized by more than one species. The authors are always grateful for the unforeseen opportunity, but we do not count on it.

So far, we've discussed the importance of knowing where to look for a target species under the prevailing circumstances. There are ways, however, to *put* the beast where you want him, and this is the subject of the next chapters.

Despite the general rules given in the text, it always pays to keep one's eyes open; now and again a creature does the unexpected and inexplicable. This normally nocturnal opossum showed up in a tree in John Wootters' backyard about 10:00 a.m. on a bright winter morning. He grabbed a camera and secured this very unusual picture. (Photo by John Wootters)

7

Calling, Baiting, Decoys, And Scent Lures

The coyote is one of the most difficult of American mammals of which to secure good photographs. When I (Wootters) first met Jerry Smith, he had never taken a coyote picture of satisfactory quality. Next morning, we both dressed in camouflage and set forth into good coyote habitat. Before the morning was over, I had placed about a dozen coyotes before his lens, some of them too close to focus a 400 mm telephoto on, and he had secured a shot which was subsequently used on a magazine cover.

And how did I work this magic on the smartest of all American wild animals? Simple! I used the amplified, tape recorded cry of a distressed jackrabbit and a little knowledge of coyotes. In fact, before we started calling at each "stand," I predicted the direction from which the coyotes were most likely to come, and positioned Jerry for the most advantageous angle. During the morning, I proved correct in these predictions on more than 80 percent of our sightings.

None of this had anything to do with any occult power over the little prairie wolves, but, in a sense, I was exercising some control over their actions. Why more wildlife photographers do not use such techniques—and there are many of them, useful on many different species—is a continuing mystery to me.

We drove along a ranch road in a brushy south Texas pasture of several thousand acres (having secured permission to take pictures there, of course, from the owner) and stopped at approximately half-mile intervals. At each stop we walked 100 to 200 yards, well out of sight of the car, in an upwind direction to a clearing of sorts in the prevalent brush of the region.

The use of a taped rabbit squeal brought this beautiful coyote on the run. Wootters was fully camouflaged and positioned in an erosion gully for better concealment, which explains the unusual low angle. This is one of Wootters' all-time favorite wildlife photographs, and represents one of only three or four times in his career when he kicked himself for not having been loaded with color slide film! (Photo by John Wootters)

The scaled quail, or "cottontop," of the southwest plainly shows the reasons for both names in this shot. (Photo by Jerry Smith)

We selected spots in the shade of bushes on the sunward side of the clearing where our camouflage would blend into the shadows, usually several yards apart. I would carry a camouflaged, 12-inch speaker about 40 feet from my position, out into the clearing, pointing the bell upwind. On the other end of the cord was an ordinary small, battery-powered tape recorder. Keeping the volume low for the first few squeals of the ersatz rabbit in case of a nearby coyote, I would gradually increase volume to the maximum level for a minute or two, and then decrease it again. The first coyote would appear, usually, within less than one minute, and it was common to see three or four at each stop.

These animals had never heard a predator call before, and the month was September, when the pups of the previous spring were both bold and innocent, and they came to the sound at a dead run. As a sidelight, it should be noted that coyotes which have been fooled with a call once are hard to fool again, for at least six months, so calling in a given area can very easily be overdone. We prefer not to call an area more than once or twice a year.

Coyotes are not the only creatures which respond to the call. So do bobcats, foxes of both red and gray species, raccoons and ringtails (at night only), and almost any other carnivores, including black bears and cougars. Hawks and owls frequently show up, too, as do many songbirds, domestic animals, and herbivores, including whitetail and mule deer and javelinas. It is assumed that these mistake the coarse bleats of a jackrabbit for the distress cries of young of their own species, especially since the authors have seen only female whitetails approach the sound and then only during the season when small fawns are in the woods.

One really never knows quite what to expect when he blows or plays a predator call, which is what makes it interesting and exciting. Coyotes and foxes usually come very quickly or not at all, and if any are within hearing you will most likely have seen all of them within 20 minutes or so. The cat family comes much more deliberately, and a full hour of calling in one spot is not too long if a bobcat photograph is what you are after.

If it is, then choose an area of generally distributed low underbrush without much clear area; cats do not like to leave cover and will come much closer to the camera if they don't have to cross an opening to do it. Coyotes, on the contrary, will run across a football field, or something equally bare, to get to a call, so set up where you can see them as far out as possible and can get your camera up and pointed in that direction before the animals get too close. All predators have exceptional eyesight, plus the ability to discriminate motionless shapes (unlike the prey animals) and the slightest movement when one is within 50 yards will usually mark the end of the episode.

Here are just a few of the brands and types of predator callers on the market, from Olt, Lindsey, Weems, Scotch, Burnham Brothers, and Johnny Stewart. These are mouth-blown instruments and require some experience to master, but they're compact and handy to keep about you even when not afield for predator pictures.
(Photo by John Wootters)

One of the most useful "masking" scents, and the least unpleasant to use, is this synthetic skunk scent, available from most sporting goods stores serving hunters. The solutions are odorless until mixed in equal proportions, they seem to "jam" a mammal's olfactory sense in some way without any lasting impairment.
(Photo by John Wootters)

Bobcats are so secretive that many people live all their lives among them and never see one during daylight hours. They come well to a predator call, however, and may be attracted by plain, old-fashioned catnip. (Photo by Jerry Smith)

The small whitetail buck was drawn
to author Wootters by simulating a
buck fight by clashing sawed-off
antlers together, and was
photographed at a few feet distance.
(Photo by Jeanne Wootters)

It goes without saying that an animal cannot respond to the call if he doesn't hear it, and he will respond more readily to one within 100 or 200 yards than to one a half-mile or more away (although he can easily hear it that far on a still day, even in timbered country). Best results come, therefore, when calling is done after careful scouting, in an area with plenty of fresh sign and, during daylight hours, within hearing of likely bedding or denning areas.

The senior author has experimented extensively with night photography of called predators, without much luck. Even when well-exposed, sharply-focused negatives were produced, which was seldom, the strobe lighting was flat and unpleasing. For photographs, we have turned to daytime calling exclusively.

A tremendous variety of calling sounds are available commercially on tape, and some of them may seem somewhat unlikely to the uninitiated. Those which the authors use most are of a young jackrabbit, a cottontail rabbit, a yellowhammer woodpecker, and a gray fox pup, available from either Johnny Stewart, Waco, Texas, or the Burnham Brothers, Marble Falls, Texas. Other sounds available, and occasionally useful, are those of shorebirds, domestic bantam hens, baby javelinas, deer fawns, baby kittens, and many others. The choice on a given day may depend upon what calls have been used in the area before (play 'em a different tune!), the species expected (cats and 'coons respond better to the higher-pitched sounds), and wind conditions. A strong wind pretty well eliminates calling as a viable technique, but some tapes have more volume or carry better against a moderate breeze.

Most predators—coyotes in particular—tend to circle the source of a call before showing themselves, and to approach from the downwind side. If there is a perceptible breeze, therefore, they will pick up the photographer's scent and it's goodbye, coyote! In addition to conventional camouflage, therefore, we need some sort of olfactory camouflage as well. This is called a masking scent, as contrasted with an attractant, or scent lure. The world's most effective masking scent is skunk scent, but the pure stuff is scarce, expensive, and must be handled approximately like nitroglycerine. A research chemist named Tex Isbell in College Station, Texas, however, has come up with the perfect solution. His product is called "Skunk Skreen" and is a two-part synthetic skunk juice which has virtually no odor until the two solutions are mixed. Then . . . jump back! A favorite way of the authors' to use Skunk Skreen is to gather three or four pieces of debris—chunks of rotting wood or tree bark—at each calling stand and apply five to ten drops from each bottle to each piece. These scent stations are then tossed out, two or three yards from the caller on the downwind side. It's neat, easy to carry securely, you never have to smell your own scent screen (unless the wind shifts!), it's readily available at most stores selling hunters' equipment and supplies, and it works. We have had both deer and coyotes within a few yards downwind which gave no sign of detecting human scent. The skunk scent itself seems not to frighten an animal, even in areas where there are no native skunks, but it appears to chemically "jam" the animal's scenting apparatus as long as he is in its presence.

There are many other kinds of calls on tape besides distress cries designed to attract predators. You can purchase tape cassettes featuring bull elk bugling, moose mating calls, crows fighting an enemy, various kinds of owls, wild turkey hens and gobblers, and many others. All are useful to the cunning wildlife photographer who understands the nature of the animal. Some are territorial appeals, attracting the same kind of animal or bird because he interprets the sound as that of an intruder in his territory. This is true of the tapes of screech owls, barred owls, and great horned owls, and they can be used to put an owl in any specific tree you want him, sometimes on the specific limb you intend.

The screech owl tape, played during the daylight hours, will also attract every songbird in the neighborhood, to whom the owl is a deadly enemy to be harrassed and fussed at at every opportunity. At dusk or at night, it will usually produce a screech owl within a minute or two, and may also attract barred owls, apparently because barred owls prey on screech owls.

Crows will fall all over themselves to get to the sound of a young crow in distress, or of a flock of crows fighting an owl or hawk, for obvious reasons.

To a bull elk in the breeding season, the bugle of another elk is "fightin' words," a challenge. He will usually answer it, thus revealing his location, and often charge it, since the bulls fight over breeding rights to cow herds. Moose respond in the same way and for the same reason to moose calls.

Similarly, whitetail bucks can be "rattled up," at least in some areas, during the peak of the rutting season, by imitating the sounds of a buck fight with a pair of sawed-off antlers, and some of the most dramatic photographs of these animals are taken in this way.

The authors prefer to use tape cassettes of all these sounds (except for antler rattling, which has never been satisfactorily recorded, in our opinion) simply because the electronic equipment leaves both hands free to manipulate a camera. However, most of the sounds can be produced with breath-operated instruments of various kinds which can be purchased at a sporting goods store and which are easier to carry. We are seldom in the field without a mouth-blown predator call tucked into a pocket, even when our primary purpose is not predator pictures.

The non-hunter may be astonished at the array of wildlife calls on sale,

The commonest example of baiting animals for the camera is in the ordinary bird-feeder in the backyard, exemplified by these American goldfinches in winter plumage. (Photo by Jerry Smith)

Corn is one of the most universally-accepted baits, attracting almost all herbivorous or omnivorous species, and many seed-eating birds and mammals, like this fox squirrel. (Photo by Jerry Smith)

This is a picture of Delilah, John Wootters' homemade styrofoam turkey hen decoy, in her natural habitat. During the spring breeding season, wild gobblers fall all over themselves to impress Delilah, who required maybe a dollar's worth of materials and a couple of hours time to create. (Photo by John Wootters)

including those for ducks, geese, wild turkeys, squirrels, doves, raccoons, predators, quail, elk, crows, and many more, and we believe most wildlife photographers are missing a bet in ignoring these invaluable tools.

Some useful sounds require no instrument. Jerry Smith is expert in producing a sound with his mouth alone which will attract bobwhite quail during the nesting season. John Wootters has seen African elephants and lions called by natives using only their mouths and hands. And every photographer, hunter, and birdwatcher should master the most useful of them all, the hand-squeak. This is done by moistening the palm of the hand and "kissing" it, sucking air sharply between the lips and hand to produce a repeated, high-pitched squeak which will get the attention of nearly any kind of bird or mammal. Songbirds flock to the sound and it works well as a short-ranged predator call in an emergency.

Many species—squirrels and bobcats, to mention a couple—will investigate any quiet, sharp clicking sound, such as can be made by tapping

This is author Wootters' experimental decoy for use with a predator call. Made from a mechanical toy, it resembles nothing in particular, but adds flopping, irregular movement to the scene to rivet the eyes of an incoming predator. (Photo by John Wootters)

together a couple of pebbles or coins. Bobcats in fact will often walk right past the speaker from which the distress cries, which attracted him in the first place, are emanating to investigate the clicking of a shutter and the whine of a motor drive or winder. Sometimes the investigation is at such close range that it may make the photographer a trifle uncomfortable.

We hope it will have become obvious by now that the use of sound to control the actions and command the presence of a great variety of wildlife has immense possibilities in the field of wildlife photography, which we just may not have even begun to explore fully. We urge you to use your imagination, to try other techniques . . . and to tell us about them when they work!

Possibly the most common method of commanding the presence of a wild animal or bird is by baiting, and the most common example is the bird-feeder in your or your neighbor's backyard. Baiting is simply the placing (or growing) of food known to be especially attractive to the desired species in a place advantageous for photography. As mentioned earlier, Wootters

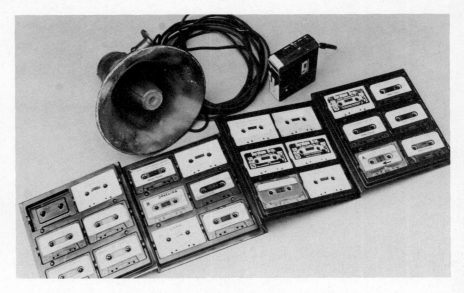

Shown here is author Wootters' cassette library of calling tapes, with a 12-inch speaker and an inexpensive tape recorder. Among the cassettes are the sounds of coyotes, deer fawns, baby javelinas, larks, shorebirds, jackrabbits, cottontails, woodpeckers, crows, owls, baby foxes, domestic hens, bull elk, and moose. All have their uses in wildlife photography. (Photo by John Wootters)

Shown here are just a few of the animal and bird calls commonly sold in stores catering to hunters. At left are two different kinds of turkey calls. Center rear are a hawk call and a quail call, followed by a mallard duck call, a whistling duck call, and a goose call. At right, a pair of crow calls. A predator call for foxes, coyotes, bobcats, and coons is at center, and the tube in foreground is an elk bugle. (Photo by John Wootters)

Author Smith waits, in full camouflage, for a predator to respond to a taped, electronic caller. (Photo by Scott Stoore)

distributes dry dog food in his backyard for the raccoons and opossums every evening, and some of the resulting photographs appear in this book. In this case and most others, it's well to take care never to put out enough food to cause the animals to become dependent upon your largess and to lose the ability to support themselves in the wild. Another important tip: *never* feed a wild animal from your hand, no matter how cute and cuddly he may seem. This is as true of a 'coon or squirrel in your yard as of the bears in Yellowstone, and if you ignore this advice, the day will come when you'll regret it; count on it!

What to feed? It depends on the animal, of course, but shelled corn, available in 50-pound sacks from most feed and garden supply stores, is attractive to an astonishing variety of birds and animals. We have fed corn to whitetail deer, javelinas, jackrabbits, ground squirrels, ducks and geese, turtles (!), cottontails, raccoons, and more kinds of birds than we have space to name. Many kinds of domestic livestock will eat it, too, so it may be necessary to place it where they cannot get at it. Maize and millet will work with most of the same species, but is more expensive.

The trick is to place the bait where the target species is likely to find it, which may not be in exactly the spot most convenient to the photographer. Put it where he passes regularly on his daily business, and, once he and his brethren have begun to visit the bait station regularly, it may be possible to move it gradually into a more advantageous position for the camera.

The cat family likes to do its own killing for the most part, and the American species, at least, usually do not respond to supplied bait. However, they may return to their own kills. Most other carnivores can be baited, especially the bears and raccoons, which frequent garbage dumps at every opportunity anyway. However, the regular providing of meat or offal is quite a chore, and an unpleasant one to boot.

Many species of mammals are attracted to salt, but, unfortunately, offering salt as bait isn't as easy as merely purchasing and locating one of the salt blocks manufactured for livestock. Few wild animals will utilize these directly, in our experience, and, of course, domestic animals will quickly eat them up. Wild game is accustomed to finding salt deposits in the earth, and that's what you have to simulate. The best way to do it is to dig a trench, dump a sack of stock salt (50 pounds) in with the earth removed, mixing the dirt and salt thoroughly before shoveling it back into the trench. If possible, wet it down thoroughly, or wait for rain to do the job. It may take as much as a year before wildlife begins to utilize your artificial salt-lick regularly, and if natural licks are available it may never happen at all. Still, in certain areas and for certain species, such a project may be well worth the effort for an enterprising photographer.

A writer who knew them well on[e] said, "A Cape buffalo always loo[ks] at you as though you owed h[im] money!," and this shot proves [his] point. These great black bulls [of] Africa are among the world['s] most dangerous anima[ls]. (Photo by John Wootter[s)]

Shots such as this whitewing dove on her nest can be set up, with care, with either a nearby blind to conceal the photographer or a camera on a tripod with remote trigger. This picture was shot hand-held. (Photo by Jerry Smith)

A baby black-chinned hummingbird that has outgrown its nest and still waits for its mother to feed him offers an unusual chance. (Photo by Jerry Smith)

This is another easy shot to set up in the backyard. Despite the speed of a hummingbird's wings, the bird itself is quite stationary in the air for relatively long periods, and prefocusing is simple. This is a rubythroat. (Photo by Jerry Smith)

This scene was set up on a deck railing in author Wootters' back-yard. The natural-looking elements were arranged carefully, a slaved strobe was set to supply a fill-in highlight, and sunflower seed was placed to attract the cardinal. Such shots can be arranged almost anywhere, with equally good results. (Photo by Jerry Smith)

Many books have been written on the subject of decoys, and there is still much we don't know about using them, especially for photographic purposes. There are many kinds, with different sorts of appeal. There are those like waterfowl decoys which suggest to gregarious species that here is a place with company and, probably, plenty of food. There are those called "confidence decoys" by the market hunters of long ago which didn't duplicate the desired species but some other kind of bird commonly seen by the desired species. An example is the great blue heron decoy set up by a duck hunter in connection with his duck decoys. Great blue herons are so alert and spooky that the presence of one reassures the ducks.

Then there is a kind of decoy that we suppose can only be called a "sex decoy," such as one which resembles a wild turkey hen and is set up in the woods during the spring breeding season to attract lustful gobblers.

Finally, the senior author has experimented with a moving decoy for use in conjunction with a predator call, which really doesn't look like anything but suggests some sort of small, furry animal thrasing around in the grass. This, made from a battery-powered child's toy, has great promise, but we still have problems to iron out before it can be considered perfected.

The possibilities in the decoy idea are endless. A major chemical company on the Texas coast is using decoys to help reestablish nesting colonies of a seabird called the black skimmer in suitable but unused sites, including an oyster-shell-covered parking lot. Our own experiments indicate that almost any kind of bird may respond to a decoy of its own kind, from a cardinal in your yard to quail and doves. A decoy is a quick way to call attention to a new feeding station, rather than allowing the birds to find it by accident.

Incidentally, the decoys really need not be too close a duplicate of the species, but can be almost stylized, only suggesting the general shape and size of the bird with the general pattern of markings. Colors should, however, be very close and must never by shiny. Even silhouettes cut from cardboard and painted are usually quite satisfactory.

If you have an artistic flair, however, inventing and trying new kinds of decoys can be a lot of fun. Wootters often uses styrofoam as a sculpturing material with excellent results, as seen in the accompanying photograph of a turkey hen decoy. One tip: if styrofoam is your medium, coat it with orange shellac and let it dry thoroughly before painting; any kind of paint or lacquer, brush-on or aerosol, will melt styrofoam. This material is a bit fragile, but otherwise quite satisfactory, being inexpensive, light in weight, and easy to work. With a couple of kitchen knives and a Surfoam-type rasp or two, almost anybody can turn out a surprisingly lifelike representation of a bird or animal in an hour or two.

In addition to being this continent's
most beautiful waterfowl, the wood
duck is a creature of seclusion and
of secret places, sylvan pools and
silent, cypress forests. This photo
of a pair of males has all that in its
subtle shadings and tranquil tone.
(Photo by Jerry Smith)

Do not be startled, however, if your decoy is subjected to savage attacks, even by members of its own "species;" remember, most birds are intensely territorial during the nesting season, and will attempt to drive away intruders of the same species while ignoring other species (except predators). An owl decoy will also be assaulted by crows, and is an essential adjunct to crow calling. Under such attack, a styrofoam fake may become battered pretty rapidly, and one of balsa wood, pine, or even papier maché may be more durable.

Decoys which can be purchased commercially include various species of ducks and geese, doves, crows, owls, and turkey hens. Almost anything else must be made by the photographer or custom-carved. However procured, decoys are another very effective way of controlling the movements of wildlife, and one which seems to be an unheard of idea to most wildlife photographers.

One more way—equally unexploited—is the use of scent lures. Unlike the masking scents mentioned earlier, these are scents designed to attract an animal to a given spot. Many are sold as commercial preparations for hunters and trappers, and can be bought in an astonishing variety of smells from supply houses catering to this clientele. Scent lures fall into two broad categories: those which smell like a favored food to the target species and those which appeal to the sex drive.

That leaves a few which must be considered unclassified (by human noses, at least), meaning that we simply don't know why an animal likes these odors. A classic example is catnip, which happens to be as interesting to wild bobcats and lynxes as it is to domestic felines. Nobody knows yet, but it might also appeal just as strongly to tigers, lions, leopards, and jaguars.

Examples of food scents are the essences of grapes, apples, or acorns peddled in sporting goods stores for deer hunters. Our results have been somewhat erratic with these, but they seem to work best, as might be expected, in areas where the deer are familiar with these foods, and when the deer are not being hunted. An absolutely obnoxious carrion odor is also bottled and is effective on coyotes, at least, and probably also on bears and other scavengers.

The sex drive scents are exemplified by some which are actually nothing more than the urine of females taken during their estrous period, and these can be absolutely devastating on males when used during the mating period. Some of these work better than others, so a little experimenting may be required in your area.

Another kind of scent lure gains its effectiveness from the fact that many mammals use urine and/or glandular secretions to mark the limits of their

Sometimes simple curiosity on the part of the subject will get a patient photographer his picture. This British Columbia ground squirrel was enticed out of its hole by the author merely by sitting motionless nearby and making a thin squeaking sound between his teeth. (Photo by John Wootters)

Certain species of birds and animals have an inherent and sometimes inexplicable comical quality about them, including bears, roadrunners . . . and jackrabbits— like this one munching on the fruit of a prickly pear cactus. (Photo by Jerry Smith)

Snow geese, Chen hyperborea,
   the ''geese of the north wind,''
lift into the wind like a blizzard.
      (Photo by Jerry Smith)

territories, an application which is one step removed from, but still related to, the sex drive. Such scents are commercially available for many kinds of furbearing mammals.

Overall, the scent lure is less successful in bringing the target animal any great distance to the photographer's outdoor "studio" (although it will occasionally do that, too) than it is in positioning him precisely where the cameraman wants him when he gets there. A squirt or a drop of lure on a tuft of grass or a small bush will almost guarantee that the critter will go to that spot and sniff at it. This means, of course, that the photographer can get the sunlight and wind direction just right, and can even be prefocused in some cases, before the subject shows up.

It may also permit him to set up a camera, prefocused and with exposure set (if not in automatic mode), covering the area in which the scent lure is deposited, and operate it by any of several remote-control mechanisms from some distance. A little deep thought will doubtless suggest a host of other situations in which advance knowledge of exactly where an animal will be standing can produce pictures which might be difficult or impossible to secure in any other way.

Most scent lures are expensive, on a per ounce basis, and very powerful, so a little goes a long way. Many of them can be diluted with distilled water without lessening their effectiveness, and the authors often apply such diluted scents with a garden-type "trigger" sprayer for wider coverage without using an excessive quantity of the precious aroma.

The use of scents is yet another technique about which we know very little, and in which there is a great deal of very exciting experimenting still to do. The whole subject of pheromones, or sex scents, is a relatively new one, being used in insect pest control but in very few other fields. Research indicates that even humans are unconsciously affected by pheromones, and the impact of these mysterious chemicals in wildlife photography has yet to be even considered.

We have discussed in this chapter methods of "controlling" wildlife's movement via the animals' eyes (decoys), noses (scents), and ears (calling). Obviously, it's often possible to combine two or even all three techniques. Calling and decoys, for example, are usually used together, as are antler rattling and scent lures on whitetail bucks. Since every creature's eyes, ears, and nose are his principal lines of defense, the more of them we can influence, or at least neutralize, the better chance we have to get him within camera range. All of these techniques, by the way, lend themselves to photographs of animals *doing* something, besides staring suspiciously or in astonishment at the camera, about which we will have more to say in the next chapter.

8

How To Be Invisible

Astandard device used by wildlife photographers since the earliest days of this fascinating pastime has been the blind, or "hide," as our British cousins call it. Their word is really more descriptive, since it's nothing more than a place to hide from our wild subjects. There is, however, more to locating, building, and using blinds than meets the eye.

First, it must be understood that wild animals know every detail, every bush and tree and structure, within their home territories, and they instantly know when anything has been added to or subtracted from the scene. Most non-hunting observers simply cannot accept this fact until they see it demonstrated as clearly as Wootters did once on his small ranch in east Texas. In a certain clearing where whitetail deer regularly came to feed, he routinely kept a block of mineralized stock salt for the cattle, always in exactly the same place. This was an object of a dull, nondescript brown color, about 15 inches high by eight inches square. The existing block was completely consumed on one occasion when he did not find it convenient to replace it for several weeks. Finally, he put a new block in place one afternoon and sat down, in concealment, to watch the deer. The first ones to show up were a doe and her grown fawn. The pair had not been in the clearing five minutes before the fawn spotted that salt block, and she promptly raised a great fuss, snorting and stamping and flaring her tail. She made her mother so nervous that the pair of them departed.

Now consider all this. The little deer immediately noticed this small, motionless, drab-colored object which had not been in her environment yesterday, even though a more-or-less identical object had been in exactly the same place for years!

A well-placed blind (perhaps with a few decoys and a duck call) can get you close-ups like this one of a mallard drake stretching his wings. (Photo by Jerry Smith)

144

The photographer who wishes to place a blind in wildlife habitat, therefore, has two choices. He can simply set it up and forget about it until it has been in place long enough for the wildlife to get used to its presence and accept it as a normal part of the landscape, or he can try to make it invisible. If he wishes to use it immediately, he must attempt the latter . . . and good luck!

For such a project, natural materials gathered from the immediate surroundings are always best, especially when rocks, a fallen tree trunk, or something similar is available as a basic structure for the blind. In this hard, cruel old world, however, such happy accidents are all too seldom placed exactly right to command the necessary view, with the sun properly behind them and the wind direction such that approaching beasts will not be alarmed. It then becomes necessary to construct a framework on which to place the covering, which adds up to a lot of carpentry.

Except for a permanent location, it's easier to start with one of the lightweight, portable blinds commonly sold for hunters and to use natural materials to break up its too-regular outlines. Even when the fabric is camouflaged, some additional dressing is advisable for the very close ranges dictated by photography.

The function of a blind is to prevent the animals from seeing the human form of the photographer. Oddly enough, many things can accomplish this, one of them being an automobile. Only recently, Wootters called a wild turkey gobbler within 15 feet of a 6,000-pound Chevrolet Suburban, parked in the open, and got the best photos he has ever taken of a wild turkey. To the bird, the metal monster was meaningless.

Such results will vary with the species, however. Where deer are accustomed to seeing vehicles, it is often possible to approach them much more closely in a car than on foot, and Jerry Smith uses this method extensively. Unlike the turkey, however, a whitetail always knows the vehicle is a new addition to his habitat, even when motionless, and will be suspicious of it until it has been there long enough for him to get used to it. Also, a vehicle has many unfamiliar odors which may alert a mammal, something which wouldn't bother a turkey at all.

Both authors have tape cassette players installed in their field vehicles with outside speakers mounted under the hood or behind the front bumper. The power lines are hooked up directly to the batteries, so the players can be used with the ignitions off, and all sorts of predators and other beasts have been called within camera range of the automobiles.

In one sense, a house makes a good blind. Birds at thoughtfully positioned feeders can be photographed from the windows of a house, of course, but if you think the house isn't serving as a blind, try going outside

This whitetail buck with antlers in velvet was photographed through the branches of a blind covered with natural foliage, producing an almost surrealistic effect.
(Photo by John Wootters)

and getting the same pictures from the same distance but with no concealment.

A handy portable blind that's widely used by photographers is a small tent manufactured by a division of the Thermos Company called a "pop-tent." This is a floored, igloo-shaped tent supported by internal, flexible plastic rods and which needs no staking. The smallest size is about six feet in diameter and light enough to pick up and move around with one hand, even when erected. Some users cut additional holes through which to stick long lenses, or camouflage the tent with spray paint, but it makes a comfortable and long-lasting blind just as it is. Being enclosed at the top, a pop-tent does get a little close in hot weather, however.

Most mammals are not accustomed to looking *up* for danger, so a platform in a tree above the eye level of the target species makes a surprisingly satisfactory "hide." An elevated position also puts the photographer's scent stream above the nostrils of the subjects. Many of us find the angle of a wildlife picture taken from an elevated blind unpleasant, but that's a purely subjective esthetic judgment.

Where there is a danger of the photographer being observed by his intended subjects as he approaches his blind, there's a trick you should know. Have a companion accompany you to the blind, and, when you're safely inside, walk away. Animals can't count, and will not suspect that more people approached than departed. Otherwise, they may steer well clear of the blind even though they cannot see you inside.

The wearing of camouflage clothing actually makes a photographer into a one-man, walking blind. Relatively few wildlife photographers take advantage of this fact, but you will notice that all bowhunters, who must get about as close to their game as a photographer, practically live in camouflage. The reason is that we need all the help we can get against the sharp eyes of wildlife, and camouflage shifts the odds a little in our favor.

The most common mistake made in relation to camouflage is leaving the face and hands bare. The Caucasian face, however, shines in the woods like a dead mackerel in the moonlight, and may attract the attention of an animal several hundred yards away. There are two solutions. The first is to camouflage the skin of your face and hands with cold cream-based makeup especially made for the purpose, and available at archery supply stores. Some brands even have an insect repellent included in the formula. If you opt for this solution, do not forget your eyelids, else you'll "blink white." The other solution is the wearing of camouflaged gloves and a headnet. The headnets are available at most stores which sell camouflage clothing, but the gloves almost have to be made at home, using leather dyes or colored felt-tip markers to paint a pair of snug-fitting buckskin or pigskin gloves.

This wild turkey gobbler was called within 15 feet of a large automobile in the open. The motionless machine meant nothing to the bird in the fervor of the mating season and served successfully as a blind. (Photo by John Wootters)

Smith dislikes manipulating camera gear with gloves; Wootters has no trouble with the controls.

A human dressed in camouflage from head to toe may be hard to see, but he still has an outline and will be instantly identified merely by his shape by most kinds of birds and animals unless he uses the available brush, light, and shadows correctly. Never allow yourself to be silhouetted, and avoid back and side-lighting which can rim-light your head, shoulders, and arms. Try always to have a little undergrowth behind you, so that your camouflage can blend your shape into the surroundings. Dappled, broken shade is a perfect place to sit or stand. Try to keep your camouflaged clothing bright and fresh; dull, faded camouflage patterns lose their effectiveness. Try to buy clothing which matches the areas in which you will wear it in tone and color; for creatures with color perception, a brown and tan pattern may work better in wintertime, while a green and brown pattern is just right for the summer foliage.

In many areas, wildlife is relatively accustomed to the passage or presence of automobiles, and can be approached much more closely in a vehicle than by a man on foot. Here, Jerry Smith uses this technique to get within range of a pair or chital bucks. (Photo by Mike Alebis)

This is a commercially-manufactured, portable blind in use. It weighs less than five pounds, complete, and is extremely durable in exposure to weather and sunlight. The camouflage covering is available in either green-on-brown or brown-on-tan colors; the latter is best for most wintertime work. (Photo by John Wootters)

Here we see Jerry Smith entering a blind which proves that a blind needn't be inconspicuous, provided it's been in place long enough for wildlife to become accustomed to its presence. On some species, however, the high angle from this elevated blind is undesirable, in the authors' opinion.
(Photo by Mike Alebis)

150

It's quite a thrill to have wild animals within a few feet of you and apparently unable to see you, which is what correctly worn and used camouflage can do for you. All of us have daydreamed of the pleasures of being invisible in the forest so we can watch the wild creatures going about their lives undisturbed, and camouflage comes as close to that magical vanishing point as we are likely to get.

If camouflage seems to be too much trouble, our only other advice is to wear dark, neutral colored clothing in browns and greens and a broad-brimmed hat or billed cap that shades your face. And stay in the car as much as possible!

The current vogue in cameras is an all-black finish, with very little white metal showing, and that's all to the good in wildlife photography. If yours is a bit too chrome-plated, it's no great trick to camouflage it with scraps of cloth from a worn-out camouflage shirt and held in place with black electrician's tape, and we believe it's well worth the effort.

No matter to what lengths you go to be invisible, most animals will spot you instantly if you make quick movements. Such species as deer, for example, seem unable to perceive an absolutely motionless human for what he is, no matter what he's wearing, but will pick up the flash of a bird's wing at 200 yards. This is probably more a matter of the mode of image formation in the animal's brain than in his retinas, but, however that may be, sudden movements are poison around almost any kind of wildlife. Avoid movement if possible, and where it isn't possible, make it slow and smooth.

There is one more way to frighten animals, even when motionless and fully camouflaged with the wind in your favor, and that is to look them in the eye! Direct, eye-to-eye contact seems to be absolutely terrifying to prey animals, at least, and unnerving to any kind, even domestic species. Try staring your dog or friend's in the eye sometime, and you'll see what we mean. He will quickly become nervous under your steady gaze, usually refusing to meet it after a minute or two and probably moving away from your presence. In some cases he may become actively hostile, growling and snarling. A direct, unblinking stare seems to be an act of aggression in the animal world, and is clearly associated with predators in the minds of most herbivores.

The portrait of a wildlife photographer in action shows all the elements of good camouflage practice: complete coverage, including hands, face, and camera, and correct use of sun direction and broken shadow. (Photo by John Wootters)

Sunglasses—preferably *not* the half-silvered kind—can conceal the photographer's eyes, and can make the difference with game at close ranges. Otherwise, keep your eyes averted, watching your subjects with your peripheral vision . . . or, of course, through your camera lens. It is not impossible that a lens is interpreted by some animals as a giant eye, staring at them, but we don't know what to do about it except to stay in the shadows or out of sight.

9

Tricks, Tips, And Techniques

*E*very "how-to" book has to have a catch-all chapter, and this is it, a few pages of useful items which neither fit in with each other nor with any other portion of the book.

The first topic is camera traps for wildlife. It happens that the very first wildlife photograph ever taken by Wootters was taken with a Kodak 620 Brownie, a fixed-focus, fixed-exposure box camera, of a fox squirrel. The camera shutter was tripped by a mousetrap which, in turn, was tripped by a string attached to a shelled pecan meat. That momentous event occurred during the early years of World War II, but the author still uses a modified mousetrap as a camera trigger 40 years later. It's simple, reliable, and cheap. A glance at the accompanying photos will reveal how the trap is modified to operate a cable release. It's even easier to rig it to close a switch and operate the solenoid which is built into many motor drives and winders.

The advantage of an automatic trigger for a camera is that it allows the subject to take its own picture, often while the photographer is at home, in bed. A trail or feeding station can be monitored continuously without the photographer having to spend long hours in all kinds of weather, cramped and silent. The disadvantage, of course, is that the camera simply records what's in front of it, at the instant the trigger is tripped. It cannot compose the picture or select the proper time to fire, so what results is a kind of catch-as-catch-can photograph which can be really excellent only by chance.

Nevertheless, most hobbyists find camera trapping exciting and fun, and occasionally a prize-winning negative will result. There is a sense of antic-

Most smaller subjects—reptiles, amphibians, and insects—are usually photographed in indoor studio set-ups where both the subject and the lighting can be controlled, but an alert photographer will find a few opportunities like this one "in habitat" in the back yard. The lizard is a green anole, and the cameraman is a Jerry Smith. (Photo by Mike Alebis)

This close-up shows how a 29¢ mouse trap can be modified as a trigger for a camera trap, for use in conjunction with a cable release. The trip-line is monofilament fishing line. (Photo by John Wootters)

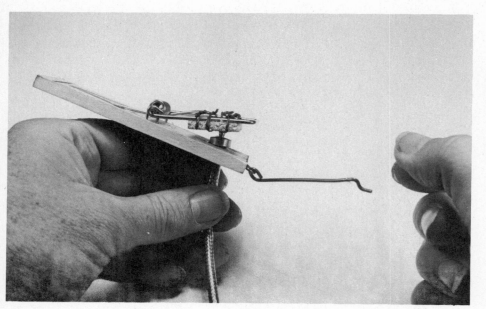

In this view the trap has been sprung, depressing the cable-release plunger. In some cases, it may be desirable to glue a small block of wood in place to limit the length of the cable-release stroke to avoid possible damage to the camera. (Photo by John Wootters)

ipation and suspense while waiting for the films to come out of the fixing bath (or back from the processor) which can hardly be matched; you don't even know what species will appear, much less in what pose it was caught.

Most camera trapping is done at night, but with modern, automatic exposure cameras there's no reason it cannot be just as successful during the day. By day or night, the sophisticated equipment available to the wildlife photographer today makes many things possible which would have seemed miraculous to the pioneer of nighttime wildlife photography, George Shiras III, back in the 1920s and '30s. He used flash powder and clumsy, large-format cameras, but he secured photos which won world-wide acclaim. To see them, the reader is referred to a two-volume set of books entitled *Hunting Wild Life With Camera and Flashlight,* published by the National Geographic Society (Second Edition, 1936). Shiras' results are easy to duplicate, or even improve upon, today with automatic thyristor strobes, inexpensive slave units, and 35 mm SLR cameras with motor driven winders.

With the proper kind of trigger (self-resetting), such a rig can monitor animal activity until it runs out of film, often exposing a 36-exposure roll in a single night. Furthermore, the strobe can stop action which would be impossible in any other way, and the setup can be rigged to assure sharp focus, something that's almost impossible for a human photographer working in poor (or no) light. Finally, some totally nocturnal species, such as flying squirrels or ringtails, can be photographed naturally with a trap of this kind.

The first requirement is the trigger. The aforementioned mousetrap is a one-time-only arrangement, and it isn't much more difficult to rig a self-resetting trigger. An example is a tread-plate arrangement activated by the weight of the animal.

This is nothing more than a pair of boards, about 12 inches square, hinged together like the covers of a book at one side and held apart by a spring or square of plastic foam (of the kind used to line camera cases). A pair of electrical contacts are provided (small brass bolts work fine and are adjustable) so that the weight of the animal forces the contacts together, sending an electrical impulse to the winder or to a homemade solenoid firing mechanism. The tread plate is buried flush with the surface of the ground in a trail, and will fire the camera each time an animal of sufficient weight steps on it. With a little care, it will not appear in the resulting photographs.

Its drawbacks are that it will work only on animals of sufficient weight (depending upon its adjustments) and cannot conveniently be made to function equally well under the tread of a deer and a cottontail rabbit. Animals with a longer stride may step over it and be missed, and very heavy animals, including domestic cattle, may damage the unit.

With a little ingenuity, nearly anything is possible. Wootters had rigged a bit of bait on a length of monofilament fishing line (nearly invisible in a flash photograph) so that the bait was suspended a few inches above the ground from a springy copper wire. When the bait was tugged at, the wire bent down to make contact with another wire to send the electrical impulse. The idea is that the flash and shutter noise will scare the subject away and he will release the bait, allowing the contact to be broken. With raccoons, however, this may be a vain hope after the first shot or two.

It's important to provide for the breaking of the contact in some way, however; otherwise a continuous impulse may burn out the solenoid which actually trips the camera.

The ultimate camera trap trigger is an invisible, infrared beam of light, and just such a trigger is now being manufactured by a firm called Wilderness Electronics, Inc., in California. This gilhickey works day or night, and is very portable and easy to set up. It can be set high enough to catch only the larger animals, or low enough to photograph even the smallest (in which mode it will not be tripped by the leg of a deer breaking the beam). There is nothing to alert the animal, so the photograph will show it in a natural position. The price is undetermined on this unit as this is written, but we would imagine it will retail for something over $100.

The flat lighting from a strobe, mentioned earlier, can easily be avoided in

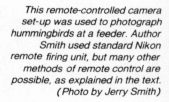

This remote-controlled camera set-up was used to photograph hummingbirds at a feeder. Author Smith used standard Nikon remote firing unit, but many other methods of remote control are possible, as explained in the text. (Photo by Jerry Smith)

a nighttime camera trap rig merely by using one or two additional strobes triggered by "slave-eye" units responding to the main flash. The only caution here is to make certain the slave units' output is less than that of the main unit, which should be an automatic one. If their total output is greater, or they are much to close to the subject, they can overpower the main unit's light sensor and result in overexposure. Their purpose is merely to wipe out harsh shadows and lend some modeling to the subject, anyway, with the principal light source remaining at the camera.

Some very dramatic action photographs are possible with a setup like this if the photographer can devise a means of startling the animal just before the main flash goes off. Such pictures might catch the subject halfway into a wild bound, for example, muscles bunched and driving. This might require two triggers, one to pop a cap-pistol cap, for example, or fire a small strobe a split-second before the exposure is made. Timing is difficult, but the results may well be worth the trouble. The ideal solution would be to rig a camera with a high-speed motor drive and rapid-recycling strobe to fire two consecutive shots with each triggering, but the authors have not yet succeeded in working out the engineering of such a mechanism.

One additional note: be sure to protect the camera and other gear against dew and possible thundershowers by wrapping with plastic, and be aware of the possibility of electrical triggering as a result of getting wet. Do not rely on a simple tripod (a startled deer might run over it) but use a clampod or other arrangement to fix the valuable equipment securely in place. If bears are on the agenda, it might even be desirable to put the camera in a steel box with a hole cut for the lens, since a couple of cameras have been known to have been eaten by black bears. An army surplus ammunition box works well and is inexpensive.

Many smaller subjects such as insects, reptiles, and amphibians are quite difficult to photograph in habitat, and most of the really good shots of such which you see are made in indoor studio situations where the subject and the lighting are more easily controlled, and a satisfactory background can be provided. Since these subjects are largely cold-blooded, their activity levels are determined by their internal body temperature. A standard technique among professionals in photographing such creatures is simply to pop them into the refrigerator for a while (in a jar or sack, of course, and be *certain* to give prior notice to the lady of the kitchen!) and cool them down. They will then be quite sluggish but still lifelike, and can be posed as you want them. The heat of photo floods will warm them up pretty quickly, however, so watch them carefully and stick them back into the cooler before they become unmanageable. Please note that we said refrigerator, and not freezer; having the body temperature lowered a couple of

The usefulness of a slave strobe trigger is illustrated here. Co-author Smith, at left, fires the master flash unit synchronized with the camera shutter. His flash triggers the slaved unit being handled by Wootters, at right, which provides some modeling and shadow relief in the resulting picture. Wootters also shines a flashlight on the raccoon ''sitter'' to help Smith focus. (Photo by Jeanne Wootters)

This shot reveals the result of the dual-strobe technique with slave trigger. A single, on-camera electronic flash would have been harsh and flat, without modeling and with heavy black shadows on the background tree. The second, weaker strobe eliminates hard shadows and yields a pleasing perspective. (Photo by John Wootters)

This is one of the pictures taken as described nearby, using a strobe on the camera only to trigger another, closer slaved electronic flash unit. The day was cloudy-dull, but the fill-in light from the slaved strobe picks up the picture nicely. (Photo by Jerry Smith)

Snakes are among the most difficult of all forms of wildlife of which to produce pictures which clearly delineate the creature's shape. Note here how the rattlesnake's body contours are distorted by the shadows even though he is on open ground. Exercise extreme caution when working with dangerous venomous reptiles like this. (Photo by John Wootters)

degrees will not harm cold-blooded animals, but being frozen obviously will.

As mentioned in the Introduction, most reptiles and amphibians are very easily killed by prolonged exposure to direct sunlight or any other heat source, since they have no physiological mechanisms for getting rid of excess heat. Better pictures and more manageable subjects result from shooting in the shade with flash fill, or in the studio with bounce-light. When photographing snakes in available light outside, put the snake down and cover it with a sack or towel while setting up and focusing. Then have an assistant gently lift the covering away. The snake will usually remain still for several seconds, but not much longer than that, so be prepared to make your exposures immediately.

Snakes in general are among the most difficult of all wildlife subjects for photography. We need not add that some of them are also among the most dangerous. The desirable close-ups demand something longer than a normal lens, but then the shape of the animal gives problems because of the narrowed depth of field of a telephoto. For the smaller, nonpoisonous species, something in the 85 to 100 mm range may work well; with the larger ones, poisonous or otherwise, a 100 mm is about minimum.

Another problem with serpents is that part of their natural camouflage comes from the closeness of their bodies to the surface upon which they are resting; the body shape is distorted and obscured by the shadows they cast. For scientific purposes, these can be eliminated by photographing the specimens on an underlit ground glass surface. For a "natural habitat" effect, however, the best results come from diffused lighting, bounce-light or open shade conditions. Such lighting also brings out the interesting textures on these beautiful creatures.

One more time, please do not handle venomous reptiles unless you *know* you know what you're doing, and do not handle snakes at all unless you are certain of your identifications. Wootters has been bitten by poisonous snakes three times in the course of ignoring this advice, and does not recommend it!

Remote photography will occasionally get you a picture you couldn't get in any other way. Again, the sophisticated equipment available to the wildlife photographer today makes it comparatively easy, the only problem being a decision on which of the many remote shutter release mechanisms to use. This depends partially upon the distances involved. Most "system" cameras include in their systems an electric remote release which works in conjunction with the drive or winder. There are also pneumatic-release accessories, in which there may be some lag, however, at the greater distances. In some of them, it's practical to insert an air pump of the sort used for bicycle tires or basketballs to get a more positive action.

Both radio-controlled and infrared-sensing releases are manufactured. They work well within their range limitations (although the radio versions can be triggered by local CB transmissions; a passing trucker asks his good buddy for a smokey report and you get a whole roll of pictures of nothing!) but they are fairly expensive. Any model airplane shop which carries radio-controlled flying models, however, can help you rig up a remote camera release a good deal cheaper than the units manufactured for this purpose.

Drives and winders with microjacks can very easily be controlled from almost any practical distance with a length of speaker wire, an eighth-inch coaxial plug available at electronics stores, a battery of correct voltage, and any kind of push-button or toggle switch, at a total cost of only a few dollars.

The value of a remote set-up is in photographing wildlife in situations wherein there is no place for a human body, or where the photographer cannot hide himself but can conceal a camouflaged camera. Birds' nests in awkward or precarious positions are good examples. Obviously, it must be a situation in which precise prefocusing is possible, and the photographer is quite certain of the exact arena within which the action will take place.

One very valuable hint in remote-controlled photography is this: rig a small strobe facing the photographer's (presumably concealed) position,

Small electronic strobe units are immensely useful in wildlife photography, especially in conjunction with "slave" triggers such as the one attached to the PC cord of the center unit or that in the case at right. At least one unit should be a variable-output, automatic, thyrister-circuitry model like the one at right, but supplementary units can—and should—be simple, inexpensive, and of modest light output. (Photo by John Wootters)

if the camera is sufficiently distant that the shutter and / or winder cannot be clearly heard the strobe will then tell you positively when the exposure was made . . . or when the CB "Red Baron" is announcing that the super-slab is clean and green! This simple expedient will save untold anguish and frustration in remote photography, take our word for it.

The little slave-eyes mentioned above have a myriad of uses. The authors cooperated in a project recently in which songbirds were being baited to a natural looking outdoors setup on a cloudy dull day, to be photographed from some distance away with long lenses. A strobe at the camera was of little or no value, so we rigged up an electronic flash unit on a slave-eye much closer to the subjects for fill light. This unit was triggered by another strobe mounted on the camera, and some outstanding results were achieved. In this case, the light source was remote-controlled, but the camera was hand-held, a very useful arrangment with a long lens.

Elsewhere in this book, you will find a photograph of the authors taking pictures of raccoons, with Smith behind the camera and Wootters hand-holding a second flash unit. Theoretically, the unit on the camera would trigger the slaved unit being manipulated by Wootters, but this picture was taken by Wootters' wife and it was her strobe which triggered the one being held by him. Hers could not have properly illuminated both the authors and

The young of all species make appealing subjects, especially when one can catch one sniffing a flower, as this javelina piglet is doing. (Photo by Jerry Smith)

their subjects in this "how-to" picture, but the slaved units did the job very nicely, and added great depth to this nighttime scene.

With a little imagination, any reader can think of a dozen ways to employ the same principles.

Underwater photography is one of the most fascinating and most specialized forms of wildlife photography. The first problem is surviving immersion, both for the photographer and the camera. For practical purposes, a snorkeler can work down to perhaps 15 to 20 feet, which is also about the limit for good pictures without the use of a flash unit. Even a trained swimmer, however, will find the necessity to surface and then swim back down to his subjects after every two or three exposures, at most—an exhausting way to shoot a roll of film.

The use of self-contained underwater breathing apparatus ("scuba") most emphatically requires professional training, and a certain degree of physical conditioning. In most areas within the U.S., a would-be diver who cannot show a "C-card," certifying successful completion of a rigorous training course in a recognized diving school, will not be allowed to dive with a reputable guide or to rent gear or buy compressed air from a dive shop. In most other nations around the Caribbean, unfortunately, such precautions are not so carefully observed and a few dollar bills substitute nicely.

Resist the impulse. Take the course and become properly certified or stay strictly away from scuba gear. It's *your* life that's being risked, not that of the cynic who rents you some tanks and a regulator without asking for a C-card.

With that out of the way, the next question is whether to invest in a water-tight housing for your regular 35 mm SLR camera, or in a camera which requires no housing, such as the Nikonos series by Nikon. The latter course of action may be the easiest and possibly the least expensive in the long run, and has been author Wootters' approach to the problem. If you choose a housing for your regular camera, remember that a mild wide-angle lens becomes, in effect, a "normal" lens underwater, due to the magnifying effect of the medium.

Except for black-and-white film, a strobe is an absolute necessity underwater, because of the high rate of absorption of light by increasing depths of water. This absorption is differential in terms of light wavelengths, the reds disappearing first as we descend, and then the yellows, until only the blue light remains. The strobe puts the phenomenal colors of underwater life back into the picture, even where it is not required, simply to get a correct exposure.

There are a few problems, however. First, the strobe simply must be mounted away from the camera; otherwise, the light will be reflected back

As a general rule, if the
photographer places the head of a
quadrupedal animal in the center of
the frame and avoids dividing the
scene in halves with the horizon, a
pleasing compositon will result.
(Photo by Jerry Smith)

to the lens from the invisible particles suspended in the water to produce an effect like snow. The solution is an aluminum bar and bracket to set the flash unit as much as 24 inches out to one side of the camera, correctly aimed, of course, to illuminate the area at which the lens is looking. Needless to say, any conventional electronic flash unit also requires a waterproof housing for use below the waves.

Next comes the fact that the diver / photographer is wearing a mask and cannot use a conventional viewfinder. Focusing must be by "guesstimate" and framing by means of some sort of sportfinder. For setting the range, the magnifying effect of the water can be ignored; it is the same for the lens as it is for your eyes, roughly.

If the camera has a through-the-lens exposure meter but no automatic exposure mode, you're out of luck; you will not be able to see the metering display. A cheap hand-held exposure meter in its own watertight housing, hung around your neck on a cord, is the solution to this one. However good you may be at judging light values by eye in your own world, you'll be badly fooled underwater. Take the meter along. Set the exposure for the ambient light and regard the flash as a fill-in light source. Now and then, on a very near subject, you may get a little overexposure, but not very often. Water absorbs light so rapidly that, except with the very fastest films, it's difficult to overexpose even when you try.

The color and variety of life on a coral reef, for example, is so enchanting that it's hard to remember to take pictures, and there is no such thing as too much film. Some of that life, however, has very effective means of defense, so we advise that you hire a diving guide who will know where the most photogenic areas are—and how to keep you out of trouble. It goes without saying that a competent diver never dives alone and, except in special circumstances, never dives at night in the open sea.

Actually, underwater wildlife photography is an appropriate subject for an entire book. What we have covered here is the merest introduction to the basics of the topic, hopefully enough to help a reader prepare for an upcoming vacation on which he intended to try his hand at taking pictures of submarine subjects. If he gets hooked—and he probably will—he will wish to consult more comprehensive and specialized sources. Most diving shops can advise him on books and equipment, and probably sell them to him, too.

That brings to mind that, so far in this tome, we have directed the reader to stores and mail-order outlets furnishing hunting, archery, trapping, electronic, diving, and model airplane supplies. Interesting! Until we have some photography shops specializing in and knowledgeable about wildlife photography, we suppose it will continue to be that way.

Underwater photography is one of the most fascinating—and most specialized—of all aspects of wildlife photography . . . as much so as if it were taking place on another planet! (Photo by John Wootters)

10

If It's Good Enough To Publish . . .

Every beginning wildlife photographer starts out with a relatively simple goal: to take a picture of an animal. The early results are almost invariably quite similar, being prints or slides in the middle of which is a different colored dot. Intense scrutiny will, with a little coaching from the photographer, usually determine the species of the dot.

"Boy, it isn't easy to get close to a deer," the photographer will exclaim, "even with a telephoto lens! How do you guys do it?" This book will serve, we hope, as an answer to that question.

Eventually, however, with perseverance and a little luck, the photographer succeeds in more fully filling the frame with a wild animal, and when a few such pictures accumulate the thought almost always creeps into the mind, "Why not sell some of these and help pay for that new 400 mm lens?"

Well, why not? Wildlife is IN, these days. More magazines are publishing more wildlife pictures in a single month than were published in a whole year 20 years ago. There is obviously a market, but the question is, how to go about selling to it.

To begin with, there *is* a market for good wildlife photos, but it is not a lucrative one. Leonard Lee Rue, probably the most-published wildlife photographer working today, recently stated that it is impossible to make a decent living exclusively in wildlife photography, and if he can't do it, nobody can do it. Nor do we know any "pros" in the field who will dispute his statement.

In the second place, there are an awful lot of professionals, semipros, and high-powered amateurs out there burning film on birds and beasts by

If you wish to sell widlife pictures, you must fit the picture to the market. This one is ideal for a hunting-oriented magazine, for example: a technically excellent shot of a magnificent trophy male of a popular game animal.
(Photo by Jerry Smith)

the ton. Photo editors, therefore, have a lot of good material from which to choose. It is not a particularly narrow market, but there is a lot of competition. It adds up to this: unless the shot is of a rare species or shows a sort of once-in-a-lifetime event in progress, it must be technically perfect to win consideration for a magazine layout, much less a magazine cover.

The first thing an editor or art director will do with your slides is slap them down on a light table and put a loupe—a magnifier of 8X to 15X—on them. If they are not sharp, razor-sharp, he loses interest in a hurry. In any picture in which the subject's eye is visible, he will use his magnifier to study the highlight which usually appears on the moist eyeball. If it is tiny and sharp-edged, the picture is sharp, even if some other portion of the creature's body is "softer" due to a shallow depth-of-field. If the highlight is diffuse but round, the picture is slightly out of focus. If it is oval or elongated, there is camera movement or subject movement in it. Apply this test to your own slides and try to be objective. Are they really, really sharp? Or just *almost* sharp? In most cases, almost is not good enough for commercial sale.

It goes without saying, of course, that the picture must be correctly exposed and reasonably well framed. Did the tip of the critter's tail or the toes of the left hind foot slip out of the picutre? If so, can it be possible to crop the scene to just a head-and-shoulders portrait, or some similar composition. Is the animal's face split by an unfortunate twig or grass stem, or are his horns or antlers lost in a maze of undergrowth behind him? Too bad.

Artistic composition may or may not be a big factor for magazine reproduction where the full frame will probably not be used anyway, but there is no doubt that any potential buyer who knows his stuff will be impressed, if only subconsciously, with a spread of slides or black-and-white prints in which the horizon or vertical elements are not allowed to divide the frame evenly and where an animal in motion is moving into and not out of the scene. Much more important is the relationship of masses in the picture, of light and shadow, and of the overall dynamism of all the elements.

A photograph is a record of a single instant in an animal's life, in which something is always happening. If what is happening is that the creature is frozen, staring in dismay at the camera, the photo is hardly more than a statement that the subject and photographer were both present. Many such pictures are bought and published, however, because of that technical perfection mentioned above. They will almost surely lose out, though, to a photo in which the subject is doing something, whatever it may be (within the limits of good taste, of course), or in which he is expressing his personality or character in some fashion. A photo of a doe and fawn staring at the camera a fraction of a second before running away may be a usable shot, but one of the same pair nuzzling each other affectionately is infinitely more

Good wildlife pictures do not depend upon rare, exotic, or colorful species. The cottontail rabbit is almost ubiquitous in the U.S., and an excellent subject for practice by beginners. (Photo by Jerry Smith)

appealing. A picture which shows how a given animal fits into and uses his environment, or how he relates to other creatures, always has an edge over the static portrait. Many wildlife shots are powerfully evocative to human nature lovers because of their mood (loneliness, tranquillity, etc.) or the attitude of the subject (dignity, hauteur, savagery, affection, lust, mischievousness, or whatever), and are likely to be winners.

These few lines cannot begin to be an instruction manual for wildlife photography, but we hope they will serve to impress the reader with the fact that there's so much more to be recorded on film than merely the physical form of the creature before the lens. Wild animals do have moods, attitudes, distinct personalities, and individual habits, and those photos which reveal these things are easy for humans to identify with and appreciate on an intuitive level. They are also the ones most likely to catch an editor's eye, if only because he sees so few of them.

The amateur who wishes to sell some of his pictures must understand his market, like any other salesman. Magazines devoted in part or wholly to hunting are only interested in photos of game species because that's what their readers want. Your cover-quality slide of an African aardvark would bounce as high as inflation at such a market, although it might really make a cover for *AUDUBON, NATURAL HISTORY,* or *NATIONAL WILDLIFE.* Furthermore, except for a special article now and then, a hunting magazine would be interested in photos of mature, antlered males and very seldom in shots of females (where the sexes can be told apart).

The only way to know the market is to study it. That means reading, or at least looking through, every issue of every magazine to which you think your shots might appeal. Every art director has his own ideas about what he likes, and every one is a little different. One may go for big-scale scenics with the animal merely one element of the picture, while another likes blazing, dramatic action, and a third prefers sequences or "picture stories." These preferences are very subtle, sometimes even unconscious, but the discerning eye can see them there in the pages of the magazines. In any professionally edited magazine, there will be a certain infinitely subtle consistency in the kinds of pictures chosen, issue after issue. Look for it, but do not try to judge from just one issue. Half a dozen consecutive issues will make it more obvious.

Of course, it you stumble into a series or a single picture in the "blockbuster" category, the action and content of which is practically unique, nearly any editor to whose publication the subject is germane will snap it up. Real blockbusters, however, are, by definition, one-of-a-kind events in any photographer's career.

Having selected a group of pictures which meet the technical and subject matter specifications for the target publication, the next step is to offer the editor a selection. If possible, let him pick the pose and scene he fancies out of 20, rather than send him the one you think is best. You will usually be surprised at which of the 20 is chosen, which means that your own first choice would have been wrong, for that editor, that day. He may be looking for a very specific action on the part of the pictured animal, perhaps to illustrate a point in the text which will accompany the photo spread.

Many editors tend to keep a fair number of freelance photographers' slides in the files, to serve as a reservoir of stock shots from which to draw. Payment, however, doesn't come until the picture is actually published, or at least selected for publication. A photographer, therefore, can find himself with hundreds or even thousands of slides out, potential sales but not producing any revenue at a given moment. This situation engenders a strong temptation to furnish the same slides (or photos) in duplicate form to several potential markets at the same time. The temptation should be resisted, since multiple submissions are an excellent way to get on a bunch of editors' black (or, at least, very dark charcoal gray) lists in a hurry. The trouble, obviously, comes when more than one editor wants the same slide at the same time. The decision as to which one gets it must be made by you, and must result in damage to your relationship with the loser.

Another temptation is to furnish several different markets with extremely similar but not quite identical slides from the same roll of film, and this one must also be resisted. Recently a photographer did just this and two different magazines ran nearly identical shots *on the cover* in the same month. The only difference was the position of the whitetail buck's head, and the pictures appeared to be part of a motor drive series. We don't know the details, but it's unlikely that photographer has sold any more pictures to either editor since, and the *faux pas* surely didn't go unnoticed by other editors and art directors, who must have marked the photographer's name well. This is *not* the way to "make a name for yourself!"

A very few freelance wildlife photographers are so versatile and widely traveled that they may have in their files almost any kind of pictures of any kind of wildlife, anywhere in the world, in color and black-and-white, at any time. But not many! For most of us, it's better to specialize in the wildlife—both game and nongame—of our particular region, and to develop the reputation as a reliable source for good pictures of those species. When an editor then finds himself looking for a certain kind of picture, the name automatically comes to mind. When he picks up the phone and dials your number, saying, "Hey, I need some shots of ducks and geese (or whatever) pronto! Can you help me?," you have just *arrived.*

This will never happen, however, if your photos are not consistently, professionally good. Editors may purchase the exceptional, spectacular, or rare photo or series from the part-timer or amateur, but every man-Jack of them is looking for regular sources of top-quality material. We think it's also a good idea to seize any opportunity to establish a personal relationship with the buyer, rather than to be merely a voiceless, faceless name stamped on the slide mounts. But making a nuisance of oneself does not endear one to busy editors, and, in the last analysis, your pictures will have to sell themselves. If they're consistently good enough, he'll be happy to make your acquaintance, at least on the telephone.

If all this sounds like selling wildlife photos as a freelancer is a tough business, you are beginning to get the picture.

There are other routes to realizing a little revenue from your wildlife photography hobby. One of them is selling to one of the photo syndicates or agencies, about which neither of the authors knows a great deal from personal experience. Such sales may be on a one-time-only fee basis or a sort of royalty basis. Another is selling to wildlife artists who use your slides for reference on animal anatomy, etc. The per slide income is minimal, but such sales are often in volume and involve pictures for which you may have no other use; in other words, culls may be acceptable in this market, provided they are well-exposed, sharply focused culls. Since most professional photographers throw away from 75 to 90 percent of every roll of slides they take, this market can be a source of "found money." The drawback, of course, is that first you must find an artist that's interested.

In dealing with any market, the beginner must make certain he understands the terms of any potential sale. Is he selling one-time publishing rights only, after which all rights revert to him, along with the slide itself? Or is he selling *all* rights in the picture? First North American rights only? Or what? A big-time, big-name photographer may be able to tell the magazine what rights he's offering for sale, but the brutal truth is that in most cases the magazine tells *him* what rights they're buying.

The same is true of payment scales. Most magazines have a fixed schedule of payment rates for black-and-white, inside color, and outside covers. Very occasionally, a rare and exceptional photograph may permit some negotiations as to fees, but the photographer must usually accept what's offered. Different magazines' pay scales for pictures do vary rather widely, however, so most of us tend to submit our best pictures to the best paying

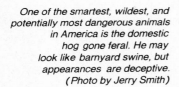

One of the smartest, wildest, and potentially most dangerous animals in America is the domestic hog gone feral. He may look like barnyard swine, but appearances are deceptive. (Photo by Jerry Smith)

markets. Freelancers who become a little too proud of their pictures, how-ever, find themselves without any markets, and we have seen this happen to some very excellent wildlife cameramen.

One hint to determined newcomers: there are a few markets around which pay little or nothing for wildlife shots, but are regarded as "prestige markets." This simply means that these publications have reputations for graphic excellence, and a photographer who's serious about getting into the business will find his own reputation enhanced by having had his stuff appear in those pages. The pay may be nil, but it's still worth his while to submit to these magazines. Many are state subsidized publications, pub-lished by the state's game and fish department, highways department, tourist department, or whatever.

How does one go about submitting to one of these or any other kind of magazine? All slides should be contained in the plastic, three-hole-punched sheets which are frosted on one side, 20 to the sheet. They should also be organized with like species and kinds together, and we like to group our "knockouts" at the top of the first sheet; that's simple salesmanship. If it's a first submission on speculation, or if the pictures have been requested by the editor or art director, the circumstances should be outlined in a brief, courteous, and to-the-point cover letter. The publishing rights offered for sale should be detailed. Every slide should have your name and address on the mount, and every print should have it on the back. An inexpensive rubber stamp will save an awful lot of writing.

Most pictures should speak for themselves; if they have to be explained or narrated, there's probably something wrong with them. However, in some unusual circumstances it may be well to add a bit of information about what's going on in the picture or how it was obtained.

The sheets of slides (or 8x10-inch prints, of which nothing smaller should be submitted) should be packaged in a sturdy mailer or manila envelope with stout corrugated cardboard backing sandwiching the pic-tures. Mail by First Class or Priority Mail, insured, and if the submission has not been requested, be certain to include return postage (preferably an SASE).

How much insurance? Since one never knows how many or which pic-ture will sell, or what it's worth, one must assume that all the slides or prints are equally valuable. We would value the package at not less than $1,000 for a sheet of 20 slides or $20 per print; some successful photographers routinely state an insured value of $5,000 or $10,000 per package, unless only a very few pictures are included.

The co-authors can add one more comment, with profound sincerity: Good luck!

Appendix

Technical Reference Sources—Films

1. "Kodak Professional Black-and-White Films" Eastman Kodak Publication F-5.

   Invaluable reference with full technical data on all Eastman monochrome films and a wealth of information on exposure, film response characteristics, and processing.

2. "Kodak Color Films for Professional Use" Eastman Kodak Publication E-77.

   Similar information on both transparency and negative color films, including those commonly used by amateurs.

3. "Kodak Darkroom Dataguide" (one each for black-&-white and color processing).

Most camera shops carry all three of these publications. Eastman also publishes annually an "Index to Kodak Information," listing more than 800 books and pamphlets. This Index is free from Eastman Kodak Company, Department 412-L, Rochester, NY 14650 (order by title and code number, L-5).

Technical Reference Sources—Equipment

Manufacturers of most SLR systems publish reference material on their products, often in book form. Camera shops often carry these for the major systems—Canon, Nikon, etc. If not, write to the manufacturer or distributor of your system for information.

Recommended Books on Nature Photography

1. "Complete Book of Nature Photography" Revised Edition, 1979 by Russ Kinne, American Photographic Book Publishing Co.

2. "Hunting With The Camera," Erwin Bauer, Winchester Press.

   This book is the best available worldwide reference on where to photograph wildlife, including Texas.

3. "The Camera Afield," Sid Latham (publisher unknown, but believed to be still in print, date about 1977).

4. "Nature Photography," Time-Life (author or authors unknown, may not be in print).

This is a fairly technical reference with great emphasis on equipment and technique.

This is, obviously, a partial listing only, of fairly recent books. Many other good volumes have been published, from which valuable tips can be gleaned, but which may not deal with the latest in equipment and films.

Recommended Books on Wildlife Behavior

1. "The Wildlife Watchers Handbook," Frank T. Hanenkrat, Winchester Press, 1977.

One of the most useful books ever published on approaching and manipulating wildlife of all kinds. A "must" for anyone interested in the subject matter of this course.

2. "The Deer of North America," Leonard Lee Rue III, Outdoor Life Books, 1978.

Rue is perhaps the top American wildlife photographer, and an accomplished hunter and lay biologist, as well. This book is written from the photographer's viewpoint, although not specifically about photographing deer. It will provide an understanding of the animal unparalleled in any other volume, however.

3. "Sportsman's Guide to Game Animals," Leonard Lee Rue III, Outdoor Life / Harper & Row, 1968.

Covers all game and several nongame mammals and describes habits and behavior.

4. "Game Birds of America," Leonard Lee Rue III, Outdoor Life / Harper & Row, 1973.

5. "Hunting Trophy Deer," John Wootters, Winchester Press, 1977.

There are too many species of birds, mammals, reptiles, amphibians, and fishes to list sources of behavioral information on all of them. The above are typical of those available on deer and other large mammals. A wealth of information has been published in various books for birdwatchers on finding, feeding, and observing songbirds, and, of course, major game species such as wild turkeys have had entire books devoted to them. We can only recommend a little library research to unearth information on habits of the species of particular interest to you at the moment. Such periodicals as *NATURAL*

HISTORY, SMITHSONIAN, TEXAS PARKS & WILDLIFE, TEXAS TROPHY HUNTERS "HUNTERS HOTLINE," NATIONAL GEOGRAPHIC, and *AUDUBON* regularly publish articles on behavioral studies on various nongame species, as do many professional biological journals.

EQUIPMENT SOURCES

Portable Blinds

1. Buck-Spin Products, Inc. (blinds and camouflage)
   6010 Kew Park
   Manitou Beach, Michigan 49253

2. Great Outdoors Products (an excellent and versatile camouflage cover)
   P.O. Box 1693
   Billings, Montana 59103

3. Sports Haven, Inc. (blinds and decoys)
   P.O. Box 88231
   Seattle, Washington 98188

4. KST Company, Thermos Division (pop tents)
   Norwich, Connecticut 06361

Decoys

1. Herter's, Inc. (all kinds of decoys, including owl, crow, turkey, dove, etc., in addition to waterfowl)
   RR 1
   Waseca, Minnesota 56093

2. R.T. Hardy (turkey hen)
   Rt. 3, Box 543
   Roanoke Rapids, North Carolina 27870

Calls, Tapes, Electronic Callers

1. Burnham Brothers (calls, tapes, players, and camouflage)
   Box 669
   912 Main St.
   Marble Falls, TX 78654

2. Johnny Stewart Wildlife Calls (calls, tapes, players; source of many unusual calling sounds, only source of owl tapes)
   Box 7954
   Waco, TX 76710

3. Philip S. Olt Co. (calls, records, accessories)
   Box 550
   Pekin, Illinois 61554

4. Scotch Game Call Co., Inc.   (best turkey gobble and mallard feeding calls
    60 Main St.   on market)
    Oakfield, New York 14125

5. M. L. Lynch Co., Inc.   (all kinds of turkey calls)
    P.O. Box 377
    Liberty, Mississippi 39645

Most larger sporting goods stores carry a selection of predator, crow, turkey, and waterfowl calls, some tapes, and other calling equipment. Examples around Houston are Oshman's, Delhomme's, Sporting Goods Inc., and Carters Country. Calls and tapes not regularly bought by hunters in this area (elk bugles, coon squallers, etc.) may have to be ordered from one of the listed makers above. Many other firms also make good calls, and one found in a store of a brand not listed above is likely to be just as good, provided the sound is OK and it's not too hard to master.

Camouflage

Most sporting goods stores mentioned above also carry a complete line of camouflage clothing, especially in late summer, as do archery equipment stores. Face-nets, gloves, caps, hats, and one and two-piece suits are usually available and can be tried on before purchase. The source listed below offers camouflage specialty items of excellent quality, such as camouflage pressure-sensitive tape, camouflage makeup (for face and hands), aerosol packaging of camouflage paints, stencils, etc.

1. Hunters Specialties, Inc.   (also some calls)
    1207 Rockford Road S.W.
    Cedar Rapids, Iowa 52404

Miscellaneous

1. Wilderness Electronics   (infrared camera trigger, soon to be
    4104 David Dr.   marketed)
    N. Highlands, California 95660

2. Skunk Skreen   (masking scent for covering human odor,
    P.O. Box CB   usually sold in better sporting goods stores)
    College Station, TX 77840

3. Safariland Archery Corp.   (Tink's #69 Doe-in-Rut Buck Lure, Tink's
    Box 579   Stink skunk scent for olfactory camouflage)
    McLean, Virginia 22101

Most so-called deer or buck lures sold in local sporting goods stores are ineffective on Texas deer. Other kinds of animal scents are available from firms selling trappers' and dog trainers' supplies, often advertised in major sporting magazines.